Praise for the first edition of *The Sisters Are Alright*

"*The Sisters Are Alright* is a love letter to black women. Winfrey Harris's unapologetic celebration of our intelligence, mettle, and beauty counters the proliferation of negative stereotypes we endure daily. She sees us, she knows us, and she also understands that we're not monolithic. Winfrey Harris surfaces stories about black women's realities that are often glossed over or tossed aside, urgently insisting with beautiful prose that contrary to our cultural narrative, black women's lives matter."

—**Jamia Wilson, Executive Director, Women, Action, and the Media**

"Tamara Winfrey Harris picks up where Ntozake Shange left off, adding an eighth color to the rainbow of *For Colored Girls*. This academic work reads like a choreopoem that challenges the notion that black women are too tough to love or be loved. The author does more than deconstruct the stereotype of Sapphire; she asserts that black women are diamonds, and she insists that her reader consider their sparkle."

—**Duchess Harris, PhD, Professor of American Studies, Macalester College, and author of *Black Feminist Politics from Kennedy to Obama***

"Tamara Winfrey Harris's book *The Sisters Are Alright* is a fitting answer to the question W. E. B. Du Bois said all black Americans are forced to consider: 'How does it feel to be a problem?' In a society that treats black people as problems and women as problems, it is nothing short of revolutionary to answer, as this book does, 'No, really, the sisters are alright.'"

—**Jarvis DeBerry, journalist, the *Times-Picayune*, NOLA.com**

"*The Sisters Are Alright* is written with the same honest, compassionate tone Tamar a Winfrey Harris is known for. This book feels like a hug for the overlooked brown girl. It's a combination of experience, honest reflection, history and popular culture, and a good read no matter your race or experience. She brings it home with a strong call to action, reminding us that while resilience is necessary, so is basic human respect—and we would do well to follow her lead."

—**Samhita Mukhopadhyay, author of *Outdated: Why Dating Is Ruining Your Love Life***

The Sisters Are Alright

Changing the Broken Narrative of Black Women in America

Second Edition

Tamara Winfrey Harris

BK®

Berrett–Koehler Publishers, Inc

Berrett-Koehler Publishers, Inc.
1333 Broadway, Suite 1000
Oakland, CA 94612-1921
Tel: (510) 817-2277
Fax: (510) 817-2278
www.bkconnection.com

ORDERING INFORMATION
Quantity sales. Special discounts are available on quantity purchases by corpora-tions, associations, and others. For details, contact the "Special Sales Department" at the Berrett-Koehler address above.
Individual sales. Berrett-Koehler publications are available through most book-stores. They can also be ordered directly from Berrett-Koehler: Tel: (800) 929-2929; Fax: (802) 864-7626; www.bkconnection.com.
Orders for college textbook / course adoption use. Please contact Berrett-Koehler: Tel: (800) 929-2929; Fax: (802) 864-7626.

Distributed to the U.S. trade and internationally by Penguin Random House Publisher Services.

Berrett-Koehler and the BK logo are registered trademarks of Berrett-Koehler Publishers, Inc.

Printed in the United States of America

Berrett-Koehler books are printed on long-lasting acid-free paper. When it is avail-able, we choose paper that has been manufactured by environmentally responsible processes. These may include using trees grown in sustainable forests, incorporating recycled paper, minimizing chlorine in bleaching, or recycling the energy produced at the paper mill.

Cataloging-in-Publication Data is available at the Library of Congress.
ISBN: 978-1-5230-9388-5

Second Edition
27 26 25 24 23 22 21   10 9 8 7 6 5 4 3 2 1

Book production by Happenstance Type-O-Rama.
Cover design: Wes Youssi, M.80 Design. Cover illustration: Adee Roberson.
Front cover photo: Jon Feingersh Photography. Author photo: Grace Miller Photography.

To Black women all over the world.
My sisters. I see you. I love you.
We will get free together.

About the Cover

Black women possess so much joy and love, yet we are told that we do not deserve this. Then there is systematic oppression keeping our access to love, respect, joy, and highest self-worth at arm's length. Through this collage I incorporated rich color, shapes, and atmosphere that aim to recontextualize this narrative. . . . Art is powerful in the way that we can create our own universe in which our dreams and visions for the future come true.

—Adee Roberson

Contents

Preface

I love Black women.

I love the Baptist church mothers in white.

I love the girls who "buss it" on TikTok.

I love the sisters with Ivy League degrees and the ones with GEDs.

I love the big mamas, ma'dears, and aunties.

I love the loc-wearing sisters who smell like shea butter.

I love the ladies of the "Divine Nine."

I love the "hot girls" in Savage Fenty, designer pumps, and premium lacefronts; and the sisters who keep a fresh Caesar.

I love the girls who jumped double Dutch and played hopscotch.

I love the *Nam-myoho-renge-kyo* chanters, the hoodoos, and the atheists.

I love the hustlers, scratching and surviving, trying to make a way out of no way.

I love the trans sisters living out loud.

I love the awkward Black girls and the quirky Black girls and the Black girls who listen to punk.

I love the "standing at the bus stop, sucking on a lollipop" 'round the way girls.

I love Black women. I love us in every way we show up in the world.

Black women have claimed and asserted our power, laying new ground for collective liberation since I wrote the first edition of *The Sisters Are Alright* in 2015. Like we always do. It ignites my spirit.

We have our first biracial Black woman as vice president of the United States.[1] And the first openly transgender Black woman serving in the Minneapolis City Council.[2] There are three Black women leading the modern civil rights movement.[3] Black women were the fastest growing group of entrepreneurs—at least until COVID-19 upended the whole world.[4] Beyoncé has broken the Internet fiftyleven times.[5] And Bill O'Reilly, who used to have so much to say about her? Fired from Fox News in 2017.[6] (O'Reilly's dismissal had nothing to do with Bey. I just wanted to provide a moment of *schadenfreude*. Or, in Black girl speak, *youhatetoseeit*.)

Black women have come a long way. We are still not free, though.

Black women organizers routinely put their lives on the line to protest violence against other bodies, while brutality against ours provokes shamefully little passion.[7] Black women with privileges, such as class, education, and light skin, have far better access to power and achievement. (Insulation from racism and misogyny sold separately.) Too many of us are poor. Too many of us don't have health care. Too many of us are or have been incarcerated. Too many of us are struggling to gain a post-secondary education or are buried under college debt. Too many of us have been assaulted. Too many of us are carrying the weight of other people's problems. The sisters are still alright—intrinsically valuable and human—*and* we are still struggling.

I have studied yoga for years and recently completed a two-hundred-hour yoga teacher training. On my mat I have found spiritual tools to navigate life as a Black woman. I also found, in a popular mantra, Sanskrit words to describe what liberation might feel like for me and my sisters. *Lokah samastah sukhino bhavantu.* May all beings be happy, healthy, safe, and free.

That sort of liberation is hard to find, because the world does not love Black women—not in the way we deserve to be loved. It doesn't truly see us. Our authentic collective and individual selves are usually hidden by racist and sexist stereotypes that we can't seem to shake—or rather, images that other folks won't let us shake.

This is confirmed for me every time I read yet another article about a little Black girl sent home from school, not for bad behavior or bad grades, but for having kinky hair; every time some well-meaning pundit or preacher offers advice to "fix" Black women to be more marriageable; every time some hack comedian tells a specious joke about tyrannical Black wives and girlfriends; every time Snoop Dogg—that is "I once walked two bare-breasted Black women on leashes down a red carpet *and* ran an actual brothel" Snoop Dogg—tut-tuts at Cardi B and Megan Thee Stallion for singing about their own "wet-ass pussy"; every time a young Black woman is shot dead by police in the night; every time the American health care system mishandles Black women's lives, leaving dead mothers and dead babies and dead Black women doctors who allegedly too "intimidated" health care professionals to receive adequate care.[8]

Misogynoir, abetted by dehumanizing caricature, is like water.[9] It fills its vessel, taking many forms, and then overflows, creeping unnoticed into the cracks of things, rotting the foundation. It spreads a belief in Black women's inherent wrongness. It decays how the government sees us, how employers see us, how the medical system sees us, how our lovers see us, how we see each other and ourselves.

I first wrote *The Sisters Are Alright* out of anger at the warped societal view of Black womanhood. I wrote it because I want Black women to be seen. *I* want to be seen. I want my three young nieces to know their own humanity and demand other people know it, too. I wrote the book because even if the world won't love us, I want Black women to love ourselves and to love each other.

I write this second edition because the Black femme experience in America continues to bend and evolve. I am a water witch, divining the places where racism and sexism flow. We need this. Otherwise, Black women's every seeming success will turn fetid.

Black women are a million different kinds of amazing. It is not our race or gender that makes this true; it is our humanity. This book is about that humanity—the textured, difficult, and beautiful humanity that lies in the hearts of all Black women. Because I love us.

The Trouble with Black Women

What is wrong with Black women? To hear some folks tell it, the answer is *everything.*

Black women are to blame for urban violence, the welfare state, and the disintegration of the Black family.[1] Media fashions them as problems and oddities or downright disrespects them. ABC News has twice convened panels to discuss Black women's lack of marriage prospects, once asking, "Why can't a successful Black woman find a man?"[2] Bill O'Reilly once claimed Beyoncé's song catalog and dance moves cause teen pregnancy.[3] *Psychology Today* published an article online explaining why Black women are "less physically attractive than other women," and during the eighty-fifth annual Academy Awards, in 2013, the satirical news site the *Onion* called African American best actress nominee Quvenzhané Wallis, then nine years old, a "cunt."[4]

Memes traded online illustrate a shocking derision for Black women. A once popular one accuses them of dropping stacks of cash on weaves and wigs, making Korean beauty-store owners rich while their own bills stay due and their children's college funds stay empty. Another compares a photo from 1968 show-ing Black women with Afros and fists righteously held high to a modern image of sisters in short-shorts and weaves twerking on the subway, as if to illustrate that all of Black womanity has lost its way.

Some high-profile Black men have critiqued, advised, and clowned sisters with little consequence to their popularity. In 2014, a viral video of a sermon by Black megachurch pastor Jamal Bryant showed the reverend in the pulpit castigating women with a line from a song by Chris Brown: "These hoes ain't loyal."[5] In a 2011 videotaped interview with now-defunct entertainment website Necole Bitchie, actor-singer Tyrese cau-tioned Black women against chasing away men with their inde-pendence.[6] Ubiquitous funnyman Kevin Hart "joked" on Twitter in 2010 that "light-skinned women usually have better credit than dark-skinned women. . . . broke ass, dark hoes."[7] And King of Comedy D. L. Hughley told a National Public Radio audience in 2012, in all seriousness, "I've never met an angrier group of people. Like Black women are angry just in general. Angry all the time."[8]

Well, damn.

Fortunately, much of this naked hatred from the 2010s sim-ply would not happen today. Folks who don't want that smoke have learned to be a little more circumspect with their misogy-noir. After portraying gross late-night caricature Virginiaca Hast-ings and implying Black women are not ready for the comedy big leagues in a 2013 TVGuide.com interview, where he claims to have been misunderstood, *Saturday Night Live* star Kenan Thomp-son told *Variety* in 2021, "I would never say anything derogatory towards Black women—like, I would never say Black women aren't funny or anything like that."[9]

(Brava, "cancel culture," teaching folks to keep that bigoted shit to themselves since 2015!)

Society and Black women's place in it have also evolved.

America is different after watching George Floyd die slowly, calling for his mother.[10] It is different after knowing police officers will not be held accountable for the bullets that hit and killed Breonna Taylor during a botched raid—only the ones that missed.[11] The pandemic and revolution of 2020 made many of us smarter about oppression and racism and equity.[12]

The cultural landscape is, if not kind, then kind*er* to Black women. This is thanks, in part, to the increased power and visibility of Black women who love their sisters and make art with that love in mind. Beyoncé sings an ode to the "brown skin girl" with "skin like pearls." Janelle Monáe insists:

> Uh, I remember when you laughed when I cut my perm off
> And you rated me a six
> I was like, "Damn"
> But even back then with the tears in my eyes
> I always knew I was the shit[13]

We *are* the shit!

Nuanced Black femme humanity is showcased in *Queen Sugar, Insecure, Lovecraft Country,* and *Sylvie's Love.* There are simply more counters to simplistic, narrow, and hateful portrayals of Black women in popular culture. (And they must be plenty convincing if the epidemic of White women masquerading as Black women is any indication. More on that later, but why does Khloe Kardashian have Beyoncé's whole face?[14] At least as of this writing . . .)

For all its many flaws, social media has also become a more powerful platform to amplify Black women's voices and push back against racist and sexist bigotry. In the wake of Kobe Bryant's death in January 2020, journalist Gayle King asked his friend and fellow basketball star Lisa Leslie, in a televised interview, how to reconcile Bryant's legacy in sports with the stain of his 2003 sexual assault charges.[15] In response, rapper Snoop Dogg took to social media, calling King a "dog-haired bitch" and threatening "back off, before we come get you."[16] Rebuke was swift. And, in little more than a week, Snoop had apologized for "just being disrespectful."[17]

(Again, don't swallow that bull about "cancel culture." "Cancellation" usually amounts to experiencing public pressure to be accountable and do better, feeling uncomfortable for a moment, and perhaps briefly losing a bag, while remaining rich and famous.)

Things are better for Black women. *Better* should not be confused with *good*. Much of the racial education that took place in 2020, when folks hunkered down in their homes reading Robin DiAngelo's *White Fragility* and Ibram X. Kendi's *How to Be an Antiracist*, did not consider the specific intersection of racism and sexism that affects Black women and girls.[18] And while the internet may be able to force a public apology, it cannot force a changed mind. Snoop Dogg apologized for calling Gayle King names; he did not apologize for implying that a Black woman who calls out sexual violence committed by a Black man is traitorous. He did not apologize for demanding Bill Cosby's release from prison, where the comedian has been since his 2018 conviction for aggravated indecent assault against a woman.[19]

Black women still have to drag Jezebel, Sapphire, and Mammy along with us into every triumph—even into the highest halls of power. Vice President of the United States Kamala Harris has been accused of sleeping her way to political success and criticized for the aggressive way she questioned opponents as a United States senator and on the Democratic presidential primary trail.[20] While she was not suitable to Democrats as a presidential candidate, she was deemed the perfect person to protect the country from the old White man voters chose instead of her.

The image of the emasculating, calculating, promiscuous, disloyal harridan still reigns in the public consciousness as the image of Black womanhood, alongside her "good" ever-self-sacrificing sister. Centuries-old stereotypes die hard.

Maligning Black women, regardless of their personal or collective truth, is part of America's DNA. The seeds for negative perceptions of African American women were planted centuries ago, when Black women were chattel, part of the engine that drove the American economy. Many scholars have named, explained, and extensively researched historical stereotypes and how they function in the lives of Black women—notably Dr. Patricia Hill Collins, in her iconic work *Black Feminist Thought: Knowledge, Consciousness, and the Politics of Empowerment*. These "controlling images," as Collins terms them, provide a template for Black women's place in public discourse. To understand how people speak about Black women today, you have to understand the source of anti–Black woman ideology.

Troublesome Roots

The moment the first Black woman set foot on American shores, sexist and racist stereotypes were laid across her back. How do you justify holding a woman as property, working her from "can see" to "can't," routinely violating her sexually and breeding her, and separating her from her children and loved ones? By crafting an image of her as subhuman—no more worthy of empathy or care than a mule. Stereotypes of Black women as asexual and servile, angry and bestial, or oversexed and lascivious were key to maintaining the subordination of Black women during slavery.

They also provided a counterbalance to the identities of middle-class and wealthy White women, who had been placed on a pedestal as perfect illustrations of femininity—beautiful, pious, pure, submissive, domestic, and in need of protection. (But still kept personally, politically, and economically powerless.)[21] Throughout this book, I frequently compare Black women's experiences with those of White women. These groups' struggles are connected by gender and yet are divided by different racial histories and privileges. I do not intend to imply that White women are primarily to blame for the oppression of Black women, or that I have forgotten the existence of Latina, Native American, Asian, and Pacific Islander women. It is simply that, in Western society, Black and White women have been placed in binary positions. White women have been idealized (through the lens of sexism), and Black women have commonly been denigrated as their opposite. Non-Black women of color tend to be racialized relative to the Black-White binary, placed in a hierarchy between the poles.[22]

There was no room for idealized femininity in antebellum cotton fields or plantation kitchens—not for the Black women consigned to work in them. Enter the three-headed hydra of distortion that clings to Black women yet today—Mammy, Sapphire, and Jezebel.

Mammy is the obedient, loyal domestic who loves most to serve her White family.[23] Unfailingly maternal, she has no personal desires and is not herself desirable; her broad, corpulent body is meant solely for work and the comfort of others.[24] Mammy is asexual, and to underscore this, she is generally depicted as dark skinned and with African features, a headscarf covering what we imagine to be nappy hair—the negative of the pale, fine-featured, light-eyed, and straight-haired Whiteness seen as the pinnacle of beauty.[25]

Of course, Mammy was always a fiction—a response to abolitionists' depictions of brutality and the ill-treatment of enslaved women. Female house slaves were not happy to be in bondage. The very idea is absurd. But the stereotype was useful in abetting slave culture. Positioning Mammy's girth and features as unattractive, particularly to White men, erased the routine rape of enslaved women.[26] The image of a content servant helped legitimize the economic exploitation of house slaves (and later the long relegation of Black women to service and domestic work).[27] Mammy also stood as the embodiment of the optimal Black female relationship to power—comfortably subservient.[28] She reinforced the idea that Black women are natural workhorses, capable of carrying multiple burdens alone—not because they have to, but out of natural ability and desire.[29]

In antebellum America, true women (read: White women) were thought too delicate for hard manual labor. Black women, by contrast, were expected to work alongside and as hard as men.[30] They were not soft and delicate in the eyes of the majority culture; they were anti-women. In the mid-twentieth century, the image of the masculinized Black woman found an identity in the form of "Sapphire," a character in the *Amos 'n' Andy* radio and television shows. By then, the stereotype had evolved into a rancorous nag—the stock angry Black woman.[31]

Sapphire doesn't know a woman's (submissive) place and is therefore emasculating and repellent to men. Not so Jezebel, the embodiment of deviant Black female sexuality. During slavery, Black women were positioned as seductive and wanton to vindicate the naked probing of the auction block and routine sexual victimization and also to justify the use of Black women to breed new human property.[32] The stereotype positioned Black women as incapable of chastity in a society that demanded the innocence of women. And it further masculinized them, ascribing an unladylike sexual hunger more typical of men.[33]

Mammy, Sapphire, and Jezebel followed Black women out of slavery, but a 1965 government report would introduce a new stereotype and cement all of these images as the cornerstones of how modern culture views Black women.

Released in the same year that President Lyndon Johnson signed the Voting Rights Act, prohibiting racial discrimination in voting after centuries of Black disenfranchisement from the democratic process, *The Negro Family: The Case for National Action* (or the Moynihan Report, for its author Daniel Patrick Moynihan, then assistant secretary of labor) put significant blame for societal problems on the role of Black women in their households:[34]

> In essence, the Negro community has been forced into a matriarchal structure which, because it is out of line with the rest of the American society, seriously retards the progress of the group as a whole, and imposes a crushing burden on the Negro male and, in consequence, on a great many Negro women as well.[35]

The Matriarch—the negative of the pleasantly nurturing Mammy—is a motherly figure who has overstepped her place and become the head of a Black family. By her failure to perform her womanly domestic duty of being subordinate to a man, we are to understand that she upsets the stability of the family, her community, and the fabric of America, leading to crime, poverty, confusion of gender roles, and moral decay.[36] In that her dominance renders her unfeminine, the Matriarch has much in common with Sapphire, and her alleged unchecked baby-making recalls Jezebel.

Here, then, is the foundation for all those news reports and "jokes" at Black women's expense. Sapphire is peeking from behind D. L. Hughley's rant about angry Black women; Jezebel is all up in Bill O'Reilly's "concern" about Queen Bey's energetic wiggling, as is Mammy in *Psychology Today*'s lament about our lack of desirability; and the Matriarch in all that late-aughts hand-wringing over the "Black marriage crisis" and advice to get Black women hitched. Emancipation may have taken place more than a century and a half ago, but America still won't let a sister be free from this coven of caricatures.

Just ask Meghan Markle. American daughter of a Black mother and White father, Markle appears to identify as a biracial woman of color and is phenotypically White presenting. That, though, is too Black for Britain's ruling class and its media lackeys. The bright and articulate former actress, self-made millionaire, global ambassador, and advocate for women and children would seem to be a valuable asset to a commonwealth of countries that includes millions of Black and Brown people. (Because of rampaging British colonialism around the globe.) But after giving up her acting career, marrying England's Prince Harry, Markle, now the Duchess of Sussex, was branded a "bully," a manipulating seductress, and asked to be 50 percent less to avoid overshadowing other members of the royal family.[37]

Sadly, the notion of Black women as oversexed, emasculating workhorses remains not just in the majority culture but deep in the bones of a Black community influenced by the broader culture's racism and sexism—as well as in the considerable rewards that come with enforcing White, middle-class, Judeo-Christian, heteronormative respectability.

Respectability politics works to counter negative views of Blackness by aggressively adopting the manners and morality that the dominant culture deems "respectable," for good or ill. In the United States of the late nineteenth century, Black activists and allies believed that acceptance and respect for African Americans would come by showing the majority culture "we are just like you." In "No Disrespect," an article in *Bitch* magazine, I explored the history of respectability politics in the Black community and how it is employed against Black women in the public eye.[38]

Black women's clubs, spearheaded by women like Ida B. Wells, uplifted the Black community and "proved" the respectability of African American women by replicating similar organizations that were led by White women.[39] Black civil rights activists showed up at marches and protests in their Sunday best, despite discomfort and sometimes only to be spat upon or stung by fire hoses. Those jackets and ties, heels, and hats sent a message: your stereotypes are untrue; we deserve equality; we, too, are respectable.[40] Dr. Sarah Jackson, a race and media studies scholar at Northeastern University in Boston, says, "Assimilation was an effective way to join the national conversation at a time when there was a great disparity in not just the visibility of Black Americans, but in the opportunity and legal protections afforded them."[41]

But respectability politics is not without its problems. It often requires an oppressed community to implicitly endorse, rather than resist, deeply flawed values, including many that form the foundation of its own oppression. For instance, newly freed Black women were expected to adhere to the strictures of the cult of true womanhood (sometimes called the cult of domesticity), a set of values associating authentic womanhood with home and family. The ideology, popular among the middle and upper classes, had long positioned White women as inherently child-like and submissive, in need of being "helped over mud puddles," as Sojourner Truth apocryphally said in her "Ain't I a Woman" speech.[42] But those restrictions were sexist and stripped White women of agency, oppressing them just as racism disempowered people of color.

The Black community still uses respectability politics as a form of resistance. And Black women carry a double burden as they are asked to uphold ideas of decency built on both racist and sexist foundations. And perhaps now more than ever—when there are so many different ways to be Black and to be a woman—this approach to liberation has the potential to harm more than uplift by reinforcing oppressive ideology and constraining the way African American women are allowed to live their lives.

Black Women Erased

The more that Americans are exposed to stereotypes about Black women in the media, pop culture, and other places, the more these stereotypes are subconsciously triggered where real Black women are concerned. This subconscious activation affects the way we are seen by potential employers, partners, the government, and others.[43] And so, Black women are perpetually forced, as Melissa Harris-Perry explains in her book *Sister Citizen*, to try to stand straight in the crooked room created by biases against us:

> When they confront race and gender stereotypes, Black women are standing in a crooked room, and they have to figure out which way is up. Bombarded with warped images of their humanity, some Black women tilt and bend themselves to fit the distortion.[44]

And some Black women angle so hard against it that they break their backs. In an effort to shake the weight of society's biased expectations, some Black women hold their tongues when they are justified in raging; deny their sexuality when they should be making love with abandon; give all their energy and care to others while they get sicker; hate African features instead of loving Black skin, broad noses, and kinks. And they make decisions not based on their particular needs and wants but to circumvent what society thinks of them.

Kawana,* a divorced mother of two, became a homemaker after she married a high school sweetheart she no longer loved to avoid being a single Black mother.

> I was tortured every day by that decision. I died inside for four years, and when I decided that I'd had enough and I couldn't live that lie anymore, everyone thought I was crazy. "Why would you leave your husband who bought you a house and a truck and provides for you?"
>
> Who the fuck said that's what I wanted? Who said that any of those things were ever important to me?[45]

When we speak in 2014, then thirty-year-old Wendi Muse is contemplating adding bright red color to her hair. Quirky style is not uncommon in New York City, where Muse lives, but she was concerned that on a Black woman, unnatural hair colors often lead to negative assessments of class and capability—more "ghetto" than "quirky and fun." She says that her race and gender make seemingly small decisions more fraught: "I police myself on the way that I dress, the way that I joke . . . I feel like I have to act really formal in spaces where others are not as guarded, because I'm constantly concerned about not being taken seriously."[46]

Erasing yourself is no good way to be seen.

The media, pop-culture critics, and brainwashed members of the Black community may think Black women are problems. In truth, African American women are seen as troubling because of the reductive way they have been viewed for hundreds of years. But Black women are not waiting to be fixed; they are fighting to be free—free to define themselves absent narratives driven by race and gender biases.

Black women know better than anyone that as a group they face significant challenges. As individuals, many Black women are struggling. More than a quarter of African American women are poor, making them twice as likely as White women to be living in poverty.[47] Black women suffer from high rates of heart disease, high blood pressure, and diabetes.[48] In a society that benefits married people, they are half as likely to marry as their White counterparts.[49] About 30 percent of Black women are victimized by intimate partner violence in their lifetimes.[50] They are, as a whole, overworked and underpaid, earning a fraction of what White and Black men do for the same work.[51] These are problems—and not the only ones. Their weight and impact cannot be diminished. But Black women should not be uniquely *defined* by their problems, nor should their problems be evaluated through the framework of stereotype.

In short, Black women are not the trouble. They are not to blame for the systemic racism, sexism, and classism that buttress societal inequities. But tackling the Goliaths of government, the corporatocracy, and American bigotry is hard. Talking about weave-wearing, mad, broke hos is much easier, although tsk-tsking Black women never made a sick body well or a neighborhood safer, improved a school system, fed and clothed a baby, or built a happy Black family.

A hyperfocus on Black women's challenges, with Mammy, the Matriarch, Sapphire, and Jezebel forever in the shadows, gives an inaccurate and narrow picture of Black women's lives. Many will never experience the struggles that are so wedded to them in popular conversation, and those who do are so much more than their weight, singleness, or thin bank accounts. The current discussion about Black women also ignores the many singular and group triumphs of Black women and erases the fact that other groups wrestle with the same ills.

The panicked headlines, the relentless criticism by talking heads and know-nothing celebrities, the bogus and biased studies, the self-righteous and snide online memes—they turn African American women into caricatures. What Black women really need is for the world, including many people who claim to love them, to recognize that they cannot be summed up so easily.

Tell the World Who You Are

"There's this quote I've seen," offers artist Lisa Myers Bulmash, forty-five when we speak, who lives in Washington State. "It says something like, 'The world will tell you who you are, until you tell the world who you are.' That includes people you think know you well. We cannot be seen as individuals with our own interior lives and motivations if others are always guessing—usually wrongly—at what makes us who we are."[52]

Forty-seven-year-old Nichelle Hayes agrees: "I think [Black women] need to hear that we're okay. We have what we need. We don't have to change. That is not to say that we shouldn't be on a path of self-improvement. Everyone should. But it's not affirming or helpful to think, 'I'm not right as I am.'"[53]

Indeed. As a Black woman and a writer committed to telling our stories, I believe it is important that we yell our real experiences above the din of roaring negative propaganda. No one can define Black women but Black women.

The Sisters Are Alright is an attempt to do just that—present a conversation about Black women by Black women. This book explores how the specters of Mammy, the Matriarch, Jezebel, and Sapphire still underpin perceptions of Black women, and it demonstrates the burden of living in the shadow of those stereotypes. But most importantly, in the following pages Black women illuminate the reality of their lives—a reality that has been too often and for too long obscured by biased news coverage, GOP dog whistling, post-racial and post-feminist progressives, and other people looking to make a fast buck reinforcing everything the world thinks is wrong with us.

Readers will also encounter rarely shared positive statistics and brief profiles of Black women who are not just alright themselves, but who are working to make sure that other Black women are alright, too. "Alright" does not mean possessing a life without hardship—being among the happy statistics rather than the dire ones. It means that Black women are neither innately damaged nor fundamentally flawed. They are simply women navigating their lives as best they can.

Many of the women interviewed for the first edition of *The Sisters Are Alright* are educated, part of the middle class, or both. And class is as great an influence on identity as race and gender. The first edition of the book also lacked the voices of trans women. I have worked to remedy these biases in the second edition. I want to tell Black women and girls' stories, delivering the truth to all those folks who got us twisted—tangled up in racist and sexist lies. I want my writing to advocate for my sisters.

All of them. But Black womanhood is so vast, there are surely still women not represented here. That is not intentional but may be evidence of my enduring blind spots. It is important to note that the women who share their stories in this book cannot represent *all* Black women. And that is also the point. Black women's lives are diverse. The diminishing mainstream portrait of Black womanhood cannot contain our multitudes.

Black women's stories look a lot different from what you've heard. And when Black women speak for themselves, the picture presented is nuanced, empowering, and hopeful.

Chapter 1

Beauty

Pretty for a Black Girl

There is a beauty revolution going down and the admiral of the Rihanna Navy is marching in the vanguard. Pop chanteuse, style icon, and giver of no fucks, Rihanna launched her Fenty makeup brand in 2017 and upended the cosmetics game, creating a "Fenty effect" that pushed beauty brands to offer a wider range of makeup shades and blew open the door to independent Black beauty brands.[1]

"It changed everything," says Patrice Grell Yursik, founder of Afrobella, a holistic beauty blog. "Now we get to see what happens when [Black women] are shifted to the center of the beauty perspective, rather than the margins."[2]

Designed with the ethos "beauty for all," the brand boasted forty different shades of foundation at launch, finally accommodating the breadth of Black skin tones, from alabaster to onyx.[3] There, promoting the brand in the debut campaign, was Slick

Woods, bald-headed, juicy lips parted to reveal an imperfectly perfect wide-gapped smile; Halimah Aden, strutting in her hijab; and Leomie Anderson, hair brushing against impossibly smooth mahogany skin.[4] Fenty included Black women and recognized their unique and diverse beauty like no other brand had before.

It's about damned time.

When I began wearing makeup as a teen in the '80s, finding the right shade was a trial. Inexpensive drugstore brands were clearly manufactured without me in mind—the deepest shade at Walgreens might accommodate a White girl with a slight tan but not my brown skin. Even the two Black department store brands, Flori Roberts and Fashion Fair, had very limited options. Nearly forty years later, Black model Nykhor Paul, who has walked the runway for Vivienne Westwood and others, was still complaining on Instagram about being ignored by the beauty industry: "Why do I have to bring my own makeup to a professional show when all the white girls don't have to do anything but show up."[5]

Naomi Wolf says in *The Beauty Myth* that "today's woman has become her 'beauty.'"[6] A certain amount of artifice has become a near imperative of walking in the world as a woman. A lash of color on the cheeks. The shaping of a brow. Makeup is a woman's most common connection to beauty. And beauty is important in a society that unfairly values women based on their attractiveness to heterosexual men.

Bre Rivera used to wear makeup, though she doesn't have a particular fondness for it and enjoys the feel of clean skin. "I understood that's what women do." As a trans woman, Bre saw makeup as a key part of survival, though she eventually gave up cosmetics, ironically, for her own safety.[7]

"[Makeup] allowed people not to see me as a trans person," she says. "You go to the store; you look cute. Other people see that you look cute. And then that invites them to want to get to know you. I found myself getting into sticky situations where I would be out and about, someone would be interested, and then I would disclose [that I am trans] and they would be, like, super [mad]."

If beauty and womanhood are symbiotic, that a $50 billion cosmetic industry has historically ignored Black women is surely illustrative of who big brands believe get to be beautiful and get to be women. The Great Black Beauty Lie is one of myriad ways America gaslights Black women. It tells them they are ugly while colonizing bits of their aesthetic and calling it beauty, replacing Black women—even in their own communities' presentations of desirable womanhood—with watered down facsimiles or sisters whose looks hew closest to the White ideal.

Never the Pretty One

Thirty-nine-year-old Heather Carper grew up in Kansas and learned at least one lesson very early: "Black girls were never the cute ones. You could be 'cute for a Black girl,' but you were never the pretty one."[8]

To be an American woman of any race is to be judged against constantly changing and arbitrary measures of attractiveness. One decade, being waif thin is in; the next, it's all about an ass with its own area code. Wake up one morning, and suddenly your lady parts "need" to be shaved smooth and your gapless thighs are all wrong. The beauty and fashion industries are dedicated to ensuring that women keep chasing an impossible ideal, like Botoxed hamsters running on the wheel of beauty standards.

But while expectations for how Western women should look have evolved over centuries, one thing has remained constant, and that is Black women's place at the bottom of the hierarchy. In

1784, Thomas Jefferson praised the skin color, "flowing hair," and "elegant symmetry of form" possessed by White people, writing that Black men prefer the comeliness of White women "as uniformly as is the preference of the [orangutan] for the Black women over those of his own species."[9] Stereotypes of Black women were designed in part to provide the antithesis to the inherent loveliness of White women, leaving other women of color to jockey for position between the poles of beauty.[10] Old beliefs die hard. Hundreds of years later, in 2011, the London School of Economics evolutionary psychologist Satoshi Kanazawa published a series of graphs and numbers at *Psychology Today*, "proving" that Black women are "far less attractive than white, Asian, and Native American women."[11] Because . . . science.

• •

Moments in Alright

Anala Beevers, age four, knew the alphabet by the time she was four months old, could count in Spanish by one and a half, and never leaves home without her US map. (She knows all the state capitals!) Anala was invited to join Mensa in 2013.[12]

• •

Neither a Beast nor Fetish Be

The inferiority of Black beauty has been reinforced partly through popular culture. In allegedly liberal Hollywood, Black women are nearly invisible as romantic partners. American fashion catwalks were so White in the early 2010s that former model and activist Bethann Hardison formed the Diversity Coalition to challenge whitewashed runways and was moved to pen an open letter to the industry:

> Eyes are on an industry that season after season watches fashion design houses consistently use one or no models of color. No matter the intention, the result is racism. Not accepting another based on the color of their skin is clearly beyond "aesthetic" when it is consistent with the designer's brand. Whether it's the decision of the designer, stylist or casting director, that decision to use basically all white models reveals a trait that is unbecoming to modern society.[13]

Since then, models of color have increased on New York Fashion Week (NYFW) catwalks. Nearly half of all models cast during the Big Apple's spring 2020 fashion week were people of color—up from under 21 percent in spring 2015.[14] But Black beauty is still marginalized, even within subcultures that pride themselves on subverting mainstream values, according to twenty-seven-year-old Black Witch,* who is active in pagan, punk, and Lolita fashion communities. Lolita fashion originated in Japan and is inspired by frilly, Victorian-era dress—lots of petticoats and delicate fabrics. Black Witch says that many of her fellow community members see Lolita femininity as at odds with Black womanhood.

"They call us ugly. They say we look uncivilized in the clothes," she says. "I once heard a person say, 'I'm not racist, but that looks like an ape in a dress.'"[15]

Increasingly, Black women are even absent in our own culture's illustrations of beauty.

"I don't really watch music videos anymore, but I have noticed that White girls are the 'it thing' now," says Liz Hurston,* thirty-four. "When hip-hop first came out, you had your video girls that looked like Keisha from down the block, and then they just started getting lighter and lighter. Eventually Black women were completely phased out and it was Latinas and biracial women. Now it's White women. On one hand, thank God we're no longer being objectified, but on the other hand, it's kind of sad, because now our beauty doesn't count at all."[16]

Seeming to confirm Liz's observation, in 2006 Kanye West told *Essence* magazine, a publication for Black women, that "If it wasn't for race mixing, there'd be no video girls. . . . Me and most of my friends like mutts [biracial women] a lot."[17]

Speaking of presidential hopeful West, his would-be First Lady Kim Kardashian is a pioneer of the galling trend of White women copying and commodifying elements of Black women's style and phenotype, benefitting from Black femme cool and carrying none of the burden.[18]

Journalist Wanna Thompson coined the term "Blackfishing" to describe White women "cosplaying" as Black women.[19] The Kardashian and Jenner sisters have long been accused of using plastic surgery, makeup, Photoshop, and elements of style, like box braids, to mimic the appearance of Black women. In fall of 2020 the internet went wild when a photo of Khloe Kardashian surfaced with brown skin, full lips, and brown hair that made her look more like Beyoncé from the Third Ward not a White girl from Calabasas.[20] Blackness is so fastened to the KarJenner empire that even Black folks frequently argue whether the sisters can rightly be called "women of color." (Robert Kardashian, Kris Jenner, and Caitlyn Jenner—parents to the sisters—are White. The late Robert Kardashian has Armenian heritage.)[21]

The Kardashians are not alone in capitalizing on Black women's style. In a 2018 Twitter thread and an article in *Paper* magazine, Thompson called out several White women influencers who had been successfully impersonating Black women on social media, gaining followings, partnerships, and brand sponsorships.

"With extensive lip fillers, dark tans and attempts to manipulate their hair texture, white women wear Black women's features like a costume," Thompson wrote. "These are the same features that, once derided by mainstream white culture, are now coveted and dictate current beauty and fashion on social media, with Black women's contributions being erased all the while."[22]

This disturbing trend reinforces that when it comes to being beautiful as a woman in America, just a dab of Blackness will do. But it puts the lie to the idea that Black women's appearance and style are deficient. If anything, they are coveted; it is only when those features and elements of style are attached to unfiltered Blackness that they become "ugly."

And in a society that judges women's value and femininity based on attractiveness, perceived ugliness can be devastating. The denigration of Black female beauty not only batters African American women's self-esteem, it also drives a wedge between Black women with lighter skin, straighter hair, and narrower features and those without those privileges.

Thirty-five-year-old Erin Millender says that the time she felt least attractive was as a teenager. "I went to a very White high school with a very J.Crew aesthetic," she says. "I was brown. I am built stocky. I've always had a butt . . . and not a tiny, little gymnast booty either. I was aware of the fact that I did not conform to the beauty standard."[23]

Erin is biracial. Her mother is Korean American and her father is Black. Many would see her light-brown skin and shiny curls and note her advantage over Black women with darker skin, broader features, and kinkier hair. But Erin says that in school she was teased for "anything that was identifiably Black. White kids don't know the difference between various grades of nap. They see frizzy hair and brown skin? That's just nappy hair to them—the same as any other kind of Black hair. Brown skin and a big booty gets 'ghetto booty.'"

But at the predominantly Black schools she attended before high school, Erin says some Black girls targeted her, jealously pulling the long hair that brought her closer to the ideal of mainstream beauty. "Then, after school, in ballet, White girls made fun of my butt."

And the attention of men like West, who fetishize biracial women, is no honor. "[It is] creepy and insulting." Erin says that far too often that appreciation comes with backhanded compliments "implying that I don't really look Black and would be less attractive if I did," plus "shade" from other Black women, "who assume I think I'm better than somebody."

Black looks are not just erased; features commonly associated with people of the African diaspora are openly denigrated in American culture. (Though it is important to note that Blackness is diverse. Black women can be freckled, ginger, and nappy; ebony skinned and fine haired; and every variation in between.)

Get the Kinks Out

Hair has been a lightning rod for enforcement of White standards of beauty. And reactions to Black women's natural hair help illustrate the broader disdain for Black appearance. While Black hair can have a variety of textures, most tends to be curly, coily, or nappy. It grows out and up and not down. It may not shine. It may be cottony or wiry. It is likely more easily styled in an Afro puff than a smooth chignon. For centuries, Black women have been told that these qualities make their hair unsightly, unprofessional, and uniquely difficult to manage.

The late Don Imus infamously called the Black women on the Rutgers University women's basketball team "nappy-headed hos."[24] In the summer of 2007, a *Glamour* magazine editor sparked outrage among many Black working women when she told an assembled group of female attorneys that wearing natural Black hair is not only improper but militant.[25] Even the US military has been ambivalent about Black women's hair. In 2014, new military grooming guidelines—since changed—provoked furor among Black servicewomen and prompted a letter to Secretary of Defense Chuck Hagel from the women of the Congressional Black Caucus. The guidelines had banned styles traditional for Black women without altered hair textures and also referred to some hair (guess whose) as "matted" and "unkempt."[26]

In 2019, the Eleventh US Circuit Court of Appeals ruled that it is legal to refuse to hire someone with dreadlocs. The Equal Employment Opportunity Commission had filed suit against Catastrophe Management Solutions of Mobile, Alabama, after that company rescinded a job offer to a Black woman who refused to cut her locs. The HR manager worried the woman's hair "might" get messy.[27]

The message that Black natural hair is innately "wrong" is one that girls receive early. In 2013, two cases of Black girls being punished at school for their natural hair made headlines. Seven-year-old Tiana Parker was sent home from an Oklahoma charter school and threatened with expulsion because her dreadlocs were deemed "faddish" and unacceptable under a school code that also banned Afros.[28] Twelve-year-old Vanessa VanDyke also faced expulsion because of her voluminous natural hair that Florida school authorities found "distracting."[29] In 2018, viral video caught eleven-year-old Faith Fennidy crying as she packed up her school bag. She had been asked to leave the classroom, told her braided hair extensions violated school rules.[30]

Is it any wonder, after generations in a society that affirms White features while disparaging those associated with Blackness, that many in the African American community have internalized negative messages about their appearance and learned that beauty requires disguising, altering, or diluting Blackness and that we pass that inferiority complex on to younger generations?

Patrice Grell Yursik does her share of counseling Black women scarred by a lifetime of beauty insecurity and parents who could not transcend their own conditioning. She shares a memorable conversation she once had with the mother of a young Black child with cerebral palsy. The woman confessed to using double the recommended amount of a caustic chemical relaxer on her daughter's hair in an effort to make it straight. The mother was distraught that despite her efforts, the child's hair held on to its kinks.[31]

"I was horrified. It made me want to cry," says Patrice. "This poor child who cannot fend for herself and cannot physically take care of herself is enduring this burning on an ongoing basis for what? So she can be what? Why are we doing this?"

It should come as no surprise that many Black women, rather than wear the braids, twists, Afros, and dreadlocs that Black hair adapts to most easily, alter their hair's natural texture chemically or with extreme heat or cover it with synthetic hair or human hair from other races of women.

Let me be clear: Black women should be free to wear their hair as they please, including straightened. But as Patrice urges, "It's really important for us to ask ourselves the tough questions. Why are we in lockstep in relaxing our hair? Why do we all come to the decision that this is something we have to do for ourselves and our children, [especially when] so many of us hate the process and see damage from it?

"Always do what makes you happy, but at least know why it's the thing that makes you happy."

During the "Black is beautiful" 1970s, many Black women embraced their natural kinks, but that rebellion gave way to assimilation in the Reagan era. The popularity of neo-soul music in the late 1990s and early 2000s, with its iconic faces such as Erykah Badu, Jill Scott, and Angie Stone representing for natural hair, opened the door for a new generation of women to embrace the nap.[32]

The challenge was that many would-be naturals found little support in traditional places for beauty advice, including beauty magazines (even ones catering to Black women) and professional stylists. Often, even mothers and grandmothers were of no help; the hair care that many Black women learned from their fore-mothers was solely focused on "fixing" or "taming" natural hair, not on celebrating its innate qualities. Many Black women had not seen or managed their natural texture in decades. Black beauty magazines such as *Essence* continued to mostly feature models with straightened hair. And, until the recent renaissance, education for beauticians included little to no training about the care of natural Black hair. Stylists were tested only on their ability to handle straightened Black tresses.[33]

What is profound about the natural hair revolution is that it has been driven by everyday Black women searching for a way to honor their natural features in spite of all the messages encouraging the contrary. Finding no support in the usual places, Black women created what they needed, forming communities online. Forums buzzed with women offering support and maintenance and styling techniques when family, boyfriends, and employers rejected the natural look. Women with similar hair types learned from one another's trials and errors. Naturals pored through Fotki (a precursor to Flickr) to find photos of cute natural styles on everyday women. Naturals began eschewing the preservatives and chemicals in mainstream beauty products and instead searched for natural alternatives. Black women such as Jamyla Bennu, founder of Oyin Handmade, began creating natural products in their own kitchens and selling them.[34]

"I didn't come from a family where people had [chemical relaxers]," Jamyla says. "My mom's hair is very loose; it's not like mine, so she didn't have the skills to do the cornrows and stuff like that. I was the Afro puff girl. Although it was always affirmed, there were not a lot of ideas about how to wear my natural hair."

Jamyla muddled through, finally beginning to relax her own hair in junior high school. But seeing more natural women in college opened her eyes to new options. "'Oh my gosh, *that's* what you're supposed to do with it! You can twist it. You can braid it.' I stopped perming my hair and have had natural hair ever since."

In about 1999, Jamyla began making hair products for herself "out of general craftiness." She experimented with common ingredients, like honey, coconut oil, and olive oil, that she had grown up using in her beauty routine. And, true to the ethos of the time, she shared her recipes. A freelance website designer, she eventually took a chance and began offering a few of her products online. Today, Jamyla and her partner, her husband Pierre, have not only a thriving online store but a brick-and-mortar retail space in Baltimore. And Oyin Handmade products can be found in select Target and Whole Foods stores across the country.

The natural hair movement is "an example of women deciding for themselves what's important, what's beautiful, what's natural. . . . Not only how they want to look, but what they want to use to make themselves look that way. It's a really empowering moment in Black beauty history and in beauty industry history because it's a kind of user-driven change."

Jamyla, like several other Black women, has become a successful entrepreneur through the Black beauty renaissance, but she has done so in a way that is uniquely affirming, unlike most consumer beauty brands. When my first box from Oyin arrived in the mail, it included a small container of bubble solution, two pieces of hard candy, and a card that read "Hello, Beautiful."

Jamyla says that approach comes from "myself as consumer, as a feminist, as a person who loves being Black, who loves natural hair. I was in a place of pure celebration and discovery, and so was everyone else around me. So were the people with whom I was sharing the product. It didn't even make sense to try to market as if to a deficit or a lack, because I didn't see a deficit or a lack.

"A lot of Black women grow up with so much negative messaging around their hair—not only from the marketing, which is, 'Fix it by doing X, Y and Z.'" Jamyla points out that caregivers often frame Black girls' hair as a problem from the time they are small. "Sometimes we'll get messages like, 'Oh, this stuff. It's just so hard to deal with.'

"My political feeling is that it is very serious work to love yourself as a Black person in America. I think it's an intergenerational project of transformation and healing that we are embarking on together."

Jamyla says that when she found herself with a platform to reach Black women, it was important to deliver an empowering message. "You know that this is fly, right? I know you know it's fly, I'm going to echo that to you so that you can feel a little bit stronger in knowing how fly you are."

Now, mainstream beauty and cosmetics industries are playing catch-up in the movement Black women began. Not only are homegrown brands like Oyin enjoying broad success, but major cosmetics companies have debuted lines catering to Black women who wear their hair texture unaltered. In 2014, Revlon purchased Carol's Daughter, a beauty company with roots in the natural hair movement.[35] Even Hollywood is taking notice, thanks to stylists like Felicia Leatherwood, who keeps natural heads looking good on the red carpet.[36] Her styling of actress Teyonah Parris (*Mad Men*, *WandaVision*) made all the flashbulbs pop at the 2013 Screen Actors Guild awards. Buzzfeed gushed that the actress had "the flyest hair on the red carpet."[37]

"We never thought that would happen," said Leatherwood of the attention-getting coif. And perhaps neither did Parris, when she first did what many Black women call "the big chop"—cutting off relaxed hair, usually leaving short kinks or coils. Parris told *Huffington Post*: "I cried. I cried. I was not used to seeing myself like that, I did not want to walk outside. . . . My [friend] . . . had to literally come over to my house and walk me outside because it was such an emotional experience, and it wasn't just about hair. It was what my perception of beauty was and had been for all of my life, and then I look at myself in the mirror and I'm like, 'That doesn't look like what I thought was beautiful.'"[38]

Since 2016, sales of hair relaxers are down 23 percent. And in 2021, there are many more places where Black women can see their beauty, including their hair, reflected back to them in all the different ways it flowers.

Patrice Grell Yursik, who is often called the Godmother of Brown Beauty, wonders if she would be Afrobella today if she had come of age with access to all of the brands and influencers available to young women today. "Not to say that I don't wish it existed. But I think that the lack of inspiration and available makeup and hair products forced a generation of us to become the creative force that we are now."

When Patrice went natural in 2002, she too went online for guidance and noticed a void of women who look like her tackling broader topics of beauty, including body image, skin care, makeup, and fashion.

"I'm a big girl. My hair is natural. I might have some skin problems. I'm trying to figure out what makeup looks good on me. Nobody was really holistically giving me that."

And so, in 2004, when Patrice launched Afrobella, she drew from her own journey to self-acceptance, including coming to terms with her body.

· ·

Moments in Alright

College-educated Black women are the most likely group to read a book in any format.[39]

· ·

Fierce, Fat, and Fashionable

For a country with a growing rate of obesity, America is remarkably unforgiving when it comes to fat women. Fat *Black* women have become lazy, comedy shorthand. Want to bring on the cheap laughs? Then trot out an oversized brown-skinned lady. Even better, despite her fatness and Blackness, make her think she is attractive and worthy of amorous attention. (Think Rasputia, in Eddie Murphy's film *Norbit,* or Kenan Thompson's blessedly defunct character Virginiaca on *Saturday Night Live*—hulking, sexually aggressive laughingstocks.)

"My weight has always been at the forefront of things that would weigh me down emotionally and make me feel like I was less attractive than other people," says Patrice Grell Yursik. "I've always been a big girl. When I wasn't a big girl, it was because I was bulimic."[40]

Patrice, though now a Chicagoan, grew up in a well-to-do neighborhood in Trinidad, where her friends and neighbors tended to be light skinned and thin. "I used to have to really psych myself up to go out because I would feel so unattractive next to my friends."

She hid her body under big, shapeless clothes. "I never used to wear sleeveless things. I felt very, very self-conscious of the stretch marks at the top of my arm and the fact that my arms had a little swing to them."

But one day, as she walked across her college campus in warm weather, a classmate, clad in jeans and a little sleeveless top, asked, "Aren't you hot wearing sleeves all the time?"

"I had never thought about it, because it was just my defense mechanism. [But I wondered,] 'Why do I feel the need to cover this thing up that is just a part of myself? To try and hide something that anybody could have seen anyway? Why am I trying to hide my arm fat?' I'm a big girl. I get hot, just like any other human being."

That moment began Patrice's transformation into the style maven thousands of women follow. "It was like I started to really come into my femininity and feel more comfortable with whatever that was. I had to define it on my own terms."

It is hard to reconcile beauty insecurity with the woman who took the stage at the TEDxPortofSpain event in 2013. Seeing Patrice standing on stage in a leather motorcycle jacket and long fuchsia skirt, a halo of burgundy kinks surrounding an impeccably made-up face, leaves no doubt why she is sometimes called the Godmother of Brown Beauty. She is fierce. But the message she delivered that day was even stronger: all women can be beautiful on their own terms. It is a notion that she says underpins the Black beauty revolution, which allows African American women, even those with kinky hair, large bodies, brown skin, and broad features, "a place at the table."

Many Black women have been liberated by that lesson.

Heather Carper says she feels beautiful more often now than when she was a kid in Kansas. She says part of her evolution from "pretty for a Black girl" to beautiful woman involved the realization that attractiveness is not as narrowly defined as mainstream culture would have women believe. Her mother once told her, "When you appraise art, you look for color and texture. With your skin and your hair, you will never lack either."

"The view of what makes you pretty is very dictated to you when you're younger. Whether it's the media or your peers, there is a whole lot of looking for external validation for what's pretty. You're just kind of checking in with everybody: 'Is that pretty? Is she pretty? Is this outfit pretty?' Part of getting older is that you stop checking in so much about whether what you like is cool with everyone else. You know, it may not ever be cool. But you know what? I like it. My beauty falls into that, too."[41]

Patrice says, "I always knew that there was something different about me, and I used to want to hide that difference when I was younger; to assimilate, to blend in. As I grew older,

I realized: Why am I going to fight what I am? I am made to be a beautiful woman on my own terms, why not just embrace that and be that?

"Am I going to hate myself forever . . . or am I going to be free?"[42]

Chapter 2

Sex
Wet-Ass Pussy

Strange that one of the very things that allegedly makes Black women unattractive—their bodies and the ways they differ from those of White women—is also the thing that marks them as voracious sex sirens.

Nicki Minaj dropped the eagerly awaited video to "Anaconda" in August 2014. It features a jungle theme, suggestively positioned bananas and oozing coconuts, a gold-chain bikini top, and lots and lots of ass. Over the hook to Sir Mix-a-Lot's 1992 ode to "back," Nicki bounces her chassis while rapping:

> By the way . . . what he say?
> He can tell I ain't missing no meals.
> Come through and fuck 'em in my automobile.
> Let 'em eat it with his grills and he telling me to chill.
> And he tellin' me it's real—that he love my sex appeal.
> Say he don't like 'em boney; he want something he can grab.
> So I pulled up in the Jag, Mayweather with the jab like:
> Dun-d-d-dun-dun-d-d-dun-dun.[1]

Later, she rubs her rear aggressively on rapper Drake's . . . er . . . anaconda.

Today, singing about fat asses might seem quaint. But your opinion about this video's celebration of large bottoms (and the cover for the "Anaconda" single, on which Minaj's G-stringed posterior is front and center) will likely depend on how you feel about female sexuality—especially Black female sexuality. Either Nicki Minaj set Black women back in efforts to liberate themselves from the Jezebel stereotype, ushering in an era of more graphic songs and videos. (Cue Doja Cat purring "play with my pussy but don't play with my emotions" in 2019.)[2] Or maybe Nicki and her "sons" are striking a blow for sexual freedom, illustrating that women, including Black ones, don't need to hide or limit displays of sexuality to prove they have human worth.[3]

• •

Moments in Alright

Believing that sexuality educators, therapists, counselors, and doctors must have more representation by women of color, the Women of Color Sexual Health Network is devoted to empowering and including more women of color, including Black women, in the field of sexuality, sexology, and sexual health.[4]

• •

Whether they are platinum-album-selling celebrities or everyday sisters, Black women often find that their sexuality and bodies are perceived through society's biases rather than on their own terms. Negative propaganda—from conversations about marriage rates and single mothers to memes about THOTs (That Ho Over There: dehumanizing slang for a sexually active woman) and gold diggers—is overwhelmingly bound up with beliefs about Black female sexuality.

Baby Got Back

Since the earliest days of European colonialism, the very shape of Black women's bodies has been viewed as a confirmation of our innate hypersexuality. Saartjie Baartman, the so-called Hottentot Venus, was a Khoisan South African woman who, in the late eighteenth century, was sold to Europe, where she was examined by scientists and exhibited to crowds as an oddity because of her large, round buttocks and supposedly enlarged labia.[5] In illustrations of the time, her body was routinely distorted to highlight the differences between "normal" White women and "savage" and licentious women of African descent. Baartman died penniless after society's taste for "freak shows" waned, but her sexual organs were displayed at the Musée de l'Homme in Paris until 1974.[6] Her remains were finally returned to her homeland in the Gamtoos River Valley of South Africa in 2002.[7]

Baartman is often seen to symbolize the sexist and racist ways that Black women's bodies and sexuality are perceived. Big Black bottoms have become synonymous with sex. Black female artists like Nicki Minaj are chastised for showcasing their considerable backsides in service for their own ends. Or they are disrespected: on a 2011 episode of *Live with Regis and Kelly*, Regis Philbin reached out and patted Minaj's behind without her consent.[8] Meanwhile, Black male artists—including Nelly, whose infamous "Tip Drill" video showed the artist swiping a credit card down the crack of a Black woman's behind—and White female artists such as Lily Allen, who sings, in "Hard Out Here," "Don't need to shake my ass, cause I've got a brain" while flanked by Black women shaking their asses, are defended in the name of art . . . or irony . . . or . . . just lighten up.

And nonfamous women and girls who happen to walk around in Black bodies every day? Cheryl Contee of Jack & Jill Politics asked five fellow panelists—Black women all—at a 2011 Netroots Nation conference whether they had ever been mistaken for prostitutes. Every hand on the panel went up. Her encounter, Contee says, happened as she left a dentist's office with her mother following a root canal, looking "deeply unsexy."[9]

One frightening by-product of this assumed carnality is that Black women are more vulnerable to forced sexual encounters, but they are even less likely than other women to be believed when the encounters happen.[10] In collecting information about a college date-rape scenario, researchers found that students were less likely to define an incident as rape, believe it should be reported to the police, and hold the assailant accountable if the hypothetical victim was a Black woman.[11]

Of course, not all Black women's bodies fit the stereotype created by the exploitation of Saartjie Baartman, but it is not so much bottoms but Blackness that gets African American women branded dangerously unchaste. For instance, right-wing pundit Bill O'Reilly criticized Beyoncé for "Partition," a grinding love song to the joys of back-of-the-limo fellatio. When "Mrs. Carter" dropped a surprise album in 2014, singing the praises of hot and steamy married sex, she caused a minor scandal.

"Teenage girls look up to Beyoncé, particularly girls of color," said O'Reilly. "Why would she do it when she knows the devastation that unwanted pregnancies . . . fractured families. . . . Why would Beyoncé do that?[12]

"She knows—this woman knows—that young girls are getting pregnant in the African-American community. Now it's about 70 percent out of wedlock. She knows and doesn't seem to care."[13]

He also branded the singer a "thug."[14]

Now seems a good time to point out that, two years after the first edition of this book was published, O'Reilly was ousted from Fox News following multiple allegations of sexual misconduct, including, according to the *Atlantic*, "approaching an African American woman whose desk was near his, referring to her as 'hot chocolate,' and grunting like a 'wild boar.'"[15]

O'Reilly's diatribes exemplify how negative sexual stereotypes about Black women are independent of the truth. Raised middle class in a traditional nuclear family, Beyoncé has been famous and wealthy all her adult life. She may be found on stage slinging vocal runs, but not thuggin' on the corner slinging dope. She has been with the same man since she was eighteen years old, and their child was born after they were married. Beyoncé would seem to fit the mainstream requirements for respectability. But that doesn't matter. Even a married Black woman, singing about sex *with her husband*, is a whore, a bad role model, and possibly a criminal.

At the same time, O'Reilly maligned Black girls, intimating that they are particularly promiscuous and fertile. Black girls are actually experiencing fewer teen pregnancies. According to a report by the Guttmacher Institute, the pregnancy rate among African American teenage girls declined 56 percent between 1990 and 2010.[16] The historic low in teen pregnancy and abortion across all races is credited to teens having increased access to the information and contraceptive services they need to prevent unwanted pregnancies.

Who Becomes a Feminist Icon Most?

Criticism of public displays of sexuality by Black female celebrities is just as likely to come from liberal sources. In "All Hail the Queen?," an article in the Summer 2013 issue of *Bitch* magazine, I wrote about the contradictory way that many feminists view Beyoncé's sexually charged performances and pictorials, especially in contrast to the deifying of singer Madonna as a feminist icon.[17]

Third-wave feminism is generally defined as sex-positive. It is the feminism of the SlutWalk, the antirape movement that proclaims a skimpy skirt does not equal a desire for male attention or sexual availability. Figures such as Madonna are praised as icons for challenging the idea that only male performers can be sexual and that female bodies can be used only in service of the heterosexual male gaze. But several third-wave feminists have questioned the bona fides of Beyoncé, who, it should be noted, proclaims her feminism publicly, even as many of her fellow pop stars do not.

⚬ ⚬

Moments in Alright

Tamika Felder helps other women by sharing her firsthand knowledge of human papillomavirus (HPV) and cervical cancer diagnoses. She has created an educational and social website, Cervivor, and assembled a global network of cervical cancer survivors who share their stories and serve as advocates and spokespeople.[18]

⚬ ⚬

In a January 2013 *Guardian* article titled "Beyoncé: Being Photographed in Your Underwear Doesn't Help Feminism," writer Hadley Freeman blasts the singer for posing in the February issue of *GQ* "nearly naked in seven photos, including one on the cover in which she is wearing a pair of tiny knickers and a man's shirt so cropped that her breasts are visible."[19] On the blog *Celebrity Gossip, Academic Style*, Anne Helen Petersen concurs, calling the thigh-baring, lace-meets-leather outfit Beyoncé wore during her Super Bowl XLVII halftime show an "outfit that basically taught my lesson on the way that the male gaze objectifies and fetishizes the otherwise powerful female body."[20] A commenter on the women's website Jezebel summed up the charge: "That's pretty much the Beyoncé contradiction right there. Lip service for female fans, fan service for the guys."[21]

Through a career that has included crotch grabbing, nudity, BDSM, Marilyn-Monroe fetishizing, and a 1992 book devoted to sex, Madonna has been viewed as a feminist provocateur, pushing the boundaries of acceptable femininity. (That is, of course, before she had the temerity to grow old.) But Beyoncé's use of her body is criticized as thoughtless and without value beyond male titillation, providing a modern example of the age-old racist juxtaposition of animalistic Black sexuality versus controlled, intentional, and civilized White sexuality.

Within their own communities, Black women and girls are often encouraged to keep their sexuality and bodies hidden, lest they reveal themselves to be "hos" or "fast girls" and give credence to the Jezebel stereotype.

Nojma Muhammad, a writer for the site Thy Black Man, points to highly sexualized videos like Minaj's "Anaconda" as the reason Black women are so roundly disrespected.

"We complain about the lack of respect and protection regarding Black women, but based on what WE put out there who'd want to secure and protect us? This is how we are viewed on an international stage."[22]

Muhammad invokes Saartjie Baartman. "She was their freak show. . . . Now we have women like Nicki Minaj that proudly and willingly place their bodies on display without a second thought. We've gone from Hottentot Venus by FORCE to HottenTHOT by CHOICE, and we totally disgrace the struggle, pain and memory of Sarah Baartman on a daily basis."[23]

The lesson people like Muhammad derive from Baartman's sad story is not about human agency—a woman's right to control her body—but instead that Black women ought to keep our actions chaste in public, lest someone think those racist, gawking European scientists and crowds were right after all. This message stands in direct opposition to that given implicitly and explicitly to Black men, who are often encouraged to trade on stereotypes of Black hypersexuality to underscore their virility.

In 2010, BET, which had for years shown explicit videos by Black male artists, featuring nearly naked women and references to sex, banned Ciara's "Ride," a mildly spicy video that focused on the fully clothed singer's sensual dance moves and suggestive lyrics, like "They love the way I ride it." The move was part of a bid to clean up the station's image.

"That sort of amazed me a little bit, that I had to say no to women, but someone had to be the grownup in the room," said Debra Lee, BET chairman and CEO. "I didn't ask for that job but someone had to say no and look at it from our young audience's perspective."[24]

There are no longer music TV gatekeepers to say no to sexual displays by women performers. Music lovers can watch uncensored videos on demand through YouTube and other platforms.

Some would argue that aggressive displays of sexuality by Black female performers such as Nicki Minaj, Beyoncé, and more recently, Cardi B and Megan Thee Stallion are empowering precisely because of historical perceptions of female sexuality and Black women's sexuality in America. The idea that women cannot be overt about their sexuality is rooted in sexist notions of female purity. The idea that Black women must be especially chaste to prove their worth and disprove centuries of propaganda against their sexuality is buying into racism and sexism and making the oppressed responsible for adapting to oppression—instead of demanding that society stop treating women's sexual desires differently from those of men.

Knowing that their daughters will be presumed guilty of lasciviousness until proven innocent, Black parents can hardly be blamed for teaching girls to keep any appearance of sexual desire, no matter how benign, under wraps, in the same way that they teach their sons not to give police officers or wannabe community watchmen reason to kill them.

I asked women in a Black feminist social media group to anonymously weigh in on the messages they received about sex growing up:

> Don't do it. Unless I was married, and then it was: Do it, but don't like it. I had some real cognitive dissonance going on when I discovered I LIKED it. Like, really liked it.

> Nobody talked to me about sex. Not after I was raped, not before. My friends were turning up pregnant with no understanding of why.

> My grandmother told me when I was seven that if I got pregnant she'd never talk to me again. My mother is a doctor but said nothing about sex except "Don't." . . . Sex ed was

mandatory in fourth grade. All my questions about "the mechanics" were answered, but I struggled for decades in the dating area. . . . I had my first orgasm, which I gave to myself, at twenty-nine.

Many baby boomers and Gen Xers I interviewed for the first edition of this book said that striving to maintain the appearance of respectability often drives them to misunderstand their own bodies, deny their own desires, and fail to fully enjoy sex even within the most "proper" of circumstances. (Millennials tell a different story, but more on that later.)

"We're so busy trying to guard ourselves against Jezebel, she's knocking on our bedroom door every time we fuck," says forty-five-year-old Andrea Plaid. "It's like: 'I can't be that Jezebel. I can't be that Jezebel.' We're so busy trying not to be Jezebel that we don't acknowledge our inner Jezebels and say that she's okay. That's the sad part."

Cristal Lee,* forty-three, says there were many problems in her first marriage. She and her husband married young, when they were barely twenty-three. They both came to the union with heavy childhood baggage. But an anemic sex life became the canary in the coal mine, signaling a much larger compatibility problem.

From the beginning, Cristal had been the initiator when it came to sex with her evangelical Christian husband, who was conflicted about premarital sex and ambivalent even about married intimacy. "I asked him if he married me just to make things right with the fact that we had premarital sex. He said 'No, that's not the only reason,' . . . but it helped him to feel less guilty.[25]

"I felt that something was wrong with me, because my sex drive and my lack of guilt was more dominant than his."

Like for many women, Cristal's sexuality had always been fraught, bound up in fears about pregnancy and sexual health and, as a teen, getting caught by parents—not unimportant things—but she says, "I think [we're] taught from day one, you keep your legs closed and you're not supposed to desire sex and sex is something that you give away or that's taken from you or that's done to you. . . . We're not taught that sex is pleasurable."

Her husband's idea of being a partner was about being physically present and a financial provider. Cristal needed more than that, but believing that divorce was not an option, she resigned herself: "Well, this is what my life is going to be. I found escape just through fantasy and imagination. Then one day, the idea just crystallized, 'Well, I can stay here and I can keep this family intact and I can accept what he has to offer, but I could get my needs met elsewhere.'"

She had an affair that eventually led to the dissolution of her marriage.

• •

Moments in Alright

In 2007, Dawn Crandell and Maya Haynes-Warren formed the New York City troupe Brown Girls Burlesque, in response to the absence of women of color in the art form's modern-day renaissance.[26]

• •

Today, Cristal is in a healthy and happy marriage and successfully co-parents with her ex-husband. But she wishes that Black women like herself were given permission to own their needs and desires, including their sexual ones.

"I know that my girls are probably going to have sex before they're married, and I am not going to give them grief about it. I don't want them to wait until they're married to have sex, because what if the sex was terrible? At the same time, I don't want them to have sex lightly, either.

"When I think about the Black women I know, there are very few that I feel like kindred spirits with—women whose sexuality is alive and evolving. I would love to see more women feel free to think beyond this sense of sex as obligation or a chore or something we give away or something we do to keep men, but instead to think of sex and personal satisfaction. [I am a] student of myself sexually—what pleases me . . . what I enjoy.

"There's nothing that says that we all have to be this one way—and that one way is trying to act like we don't really like sex, or truly not taking any joy in it because that's how we've been conditioned."

Choose (Wisely) Your Own Adventure

Cristal's Gen Z daughters will come of age in a very different sexual landscape.

Sexual mores continue to evolve, becoming less rigid and more progressive. Modern society is smarter and more accepting of the full range of the Kinsey scale. Baby boomers and Gen Xers are more comfortable talking sex than their parents were. And there are more women demonstrating brazen and unapologetic sexuality in popular culture.

In 2020, Cardi B and Megan Thee Stallion said "hold my Hennessy" and dropped a track that made "Anaconda" sound like a nursery rhyme.

Beat it up, nigga, catch a charge
Extra-large and extra hard
Put this pussy right in your face
Swipe your nose like a credit card
Hop on top, I wanna ride
I do a kegel while it's inside
Spit in my mouth, look in my eyes
This pussy is wet, come take a dive[27]

"WAP" spawned a sexy TikTok challenge that had hot girls and grannies humping the floor. Both Cardi and Megan are platinum-selling artists who make music about female sexual power. They brag about capturing the male gaze, but also about their own pleasure. In "Girls in the Hood," Megan warns, "I ain't lyin' 'bout my nut just to make a nigga happy."[28] And they are shamelessly mercenary, borrowing from the culture of strippers and sex workers, rebutting the pimp culture that has been popular among male hip hop stars. If anyone will commodify or gain from these ladies' bodies and prowess, it will be them. Cardi B advises in "I Do," "If they can't make you richer, they can't make you cum."[29]

It is important to note that not all sexually frank music being made by Black women is centered on the male gaze. Janelle Monáe's "PYNK" is a double-entendre-filled feminist ode to the vagina, accompanied by a video featuring women dancing in the desert clad in ruffly pink pants designed to look like labia majora and minora.[30] Monáe identifies as queer and a "free-ass motherfucker."

Society has always been willing to be titillated by women. It has not historically valued women who titillate. This has not changed. Cardi B's and Megan Thee Stallion's non-pussy-related opinions are derided. And when Megan Thee Stallion became a victim of domestic violence in 2020, she was ridiculed.[31]

Neither sexual evolution nor hip hop bravado have made navigating sexual stereotypes easier for Black women. In fact, women in their twenties and thirties share that the overtness of sexuality in modern culture is a smokescreen. It is even more complicated to stay on the "right" side of the line between "good girl" and Jezebel, despite all the "bussin' it" and talk of wet-ass pussies.

Kai Chapman,* thirty-two, came up in a church-going family and received the familiar advice not to have sex until marriage.[32] Her biological dad, a military man, and her stepfathers were equally strict. And the women in her life knew from experience that having children too early could derail a young woman's future. "We have high hopes and dreams for y'all," they would say. Those same women were also clear that, as a last resort, a woman could use sex to survive. "I heard them say multiple times, 'I will do whatever it takes to take care of you. I don't care if I got to sell it or what!' That was not a threat. That was a very real thing."

Kai's mom was intent that her daughters would know how to keep themselves sexually safe. "She made sure that we had very candid conversations about sex and everything."

That Kai's mother was committed to talking about sexual health is its own form of pushing against cultural repression, because like a lot of schools in the early aughts, her high school ditched sex ed in favor of abstinence-only education, even presenting students with a chastity pledge. It was "optional," but really, what girl would announce her intention *not* to remain chaste in front of an entire class?

While parents and teachers were preaching abstinence, urban radio was bumping music like Trillville's "Some Cut":

What it is ho, what's up (what's up)
Can a nigga get in them guts (them guts)
Cut you up like you ain't been cut (been cut)
Show your ass how to really catch a nut
(Oh, yeah, yeah)
Well give me your number and I'll call (I'll call)
And I'll follow that ass in the mall (in the mall)
Take you home, let you juggle my balls (my balls)
While I'm beating and tearing down your walls
(Oh, yeah)[33]

Appearing sexually available and skilled was becoming an imperative for young women on the heterosexual romantic market. (Among Black students at Kai's school, "gay" was an insult.) Twerking at parties was "a big deal—a way to showcase your sexual prowess" and gain boys' attention. Kai says the seeds were planted early for sex as commerce. If you wanted to feel empowered as a sexually active young woman, men would have to earn you—not necessarily with money or material things, but not necessarily *not* those things either. It was "empowerment" through access to the male gaze.

There were limits, though. "It's okay to be sexy and flirty or whatever, but when you get to the point where too many guys can say that they've been with you, then it's like . . . now you're in a whole 'nother territory."

Ho territory.

"Dudes could screw whoever they wanted to, but if a girl had multiple partners, then she's not worthy. I remember a guy saying, 'If she's had more bodies than you can count on one hand, she's a ho.' Another said, 'If she's messed with any of my friends, she's a ho.' Everybody's scale was different.

"It really puts you in a trick bag," Kai laments. "The messages were all over the place. Really, it was choose your own [sexual] adventure."

But don't choose wrong.

Thirty-year-old Goddess Honey* points out that the more brazen sexual displays that have been normalized for young women amount to traditional values disguised in a shorter skirt. "You changed your outfit, but your mindset is still the same."[34]

It was difficult for Goddess to discover her own sexuality amid a culture that centers titillation, the male gaze, and commerce, while still demanding that Black women avoid being Jezebels. She hates labels, but if prodded, Goddess identifies as pansexual and polyamorous. She is attracted to people based on personality and not gender, and she can have consensual romantic relationships with more than one person at a time. Neither of these ways of relating to partners were talked about when Goddess was coming of age.

"I just felt strange growing up," she says. "The first crush I had where I felt like I *like* liked someone . . . I was in fifth grade and it was a girl. I didn't have a sexual feeling; I just knew I liked her more than the other kids or something."

Today, Goddess identifies as polyamorous, a way of partnering that is currently "on the rise," according to a 2020 NPR report.[35] In a recent survey, one-fifth of respondents expressed some interest in ethical non-monogamy.[36] More than one woman I interviewed enjoys this combination of intimacy and freedom, though Black women are unsurprisingly scrutinized more for engaging in non-monogamous relationships.[37] Most of Goddess's friends and family weren't down for consensual open relationships. Having a relationship with more than one person was just cheating or hoing.

Goddess thought, "Maybe I shouldn't be feeling this. Something is wrong with me."

She found liberation in a brief relationship with a White man, watching how he approached sexuality, unburdened by racism and sexism. His sexuality was ultimately for his own emotional and physical gratification, not for consumption and display or to measure his value. "[White men have] this freedom where they don't have to overthink every single thing."

Black women, on the other hand, still have to lead their own private sexual revolutions to get to alright.

Put Respectability Politics in Its Place

In 2011, at the age of forty-two, Andrea Plaid walked in Coney Island's famous Mermaid Parade, accompanied by members of Brown Girls Burlesque. To the surprise of a troupe member, Andrea hit the boardwalk clad only in false eyelashes, glitter, pasties, and panties.[38]

"She looked at me and said, 'Girl, wait, you won't walk out like this.' I said, 'I thought this is how you're supposed to walk out. We're burlesque, right?' She said, 'You are so bold.'"

That boldness was hard won. Like a lot of Black women, Andrea learned early how important the appearance of chastity is for Black women, especially ones who wanted a respectable Black middle-class life like the one her mother envisioned for her daughters. But by young adulthood, Andrea had eschewed begging favor from society by restricting her own desires—sexual or otherwise.

"It was a gradual shedding," she says of letting go of respectability politics and forming her own ideas of what was right for her life and her body. That awakening was tested when she was diagnosed with human papillomavirus (HPV), a common sexually transmitted disease that can now be prevented with a vaccine.

"Oh my God! I felt horrible, because it was everything that my mom says: 'That's why you don't fuck around, because you can get diseases.'

"I was devastated and I told my fiancé at the time, 'If you don't want to marry me because of this, I would not blame you.' He said, 'Andrea, I would marry you anyway. It doesn't matter.' I cried like a baby."

Andrea points out that respectability politics not only can deny Black women pleasure but in some cases can deny them their reproductive and sexual health if they neglect to talk about sexually transmitted diseases, and their prevention and treatment, because of false morality. You can have sex one time and become infected or be promiscuous and never catch any STD. But, Andrea says, the myth of respectability says, "If you caught something, you a ho."

Andrea says that today, in middle age, she doesn't care so much about anyone's view of respectability but her own. She points out that it's not just Black female pop stars who are learning to be sexually bold. But for regular Black women, exploration of their sexuality often happens furtively, in the company of other Black women on the same journey. "When we get together with our girlfriends and we giggle and tease about who we want to do sideways in bed, we're almost shocked. It's like, 'Ah, you're a freak. Oh my God, so am I!'"

Messages about respectability aren't easy to shake, though. Andrea admits that they played in the back of her mind that summer day on the Coney Island boardwalk.

"But . . . I thought at forty-two, fuck it. I'm a more-than-grown woman at this point. Why not? I was actually proud of my body. I had lost a little bit of weight for my health and I thought, 'Why not show off my new body?' And I did it. The boardwalk was my runway.

"I think we need to put respectability politics in its place. No, you don't want to be twerking at your office, okay? But go twerk at the nightclub. That's what the nightclub is kind of for. Twerk in bed or go make your partner's body twitch. Go for it. It's your bedroom for Pete's sake. Who's looking at you?"

Chapter 3

Marriage
Witches, Thornbacks, and Sapphires

"I am fat," says queer-identified divorcee Erica Johnson.[*] "When I walk into, say, a Banana Republic . . . well, I see those clothes, but I know that store is not about me. When I see those stories on the news about Black women and marriage? Well, that's not about me either."[1]

African American women are half as likely to marry as their White counterparts, providing the foundation for a "Black marriage crisis" and allegedly the eventual destruction of the Black community.[2] And if you trust the what's-wrong-with-Black-women-and-why-won't-anyone-marry-them industrial complex, Black women may not be pretty or chaste enough to merit wifedom. But most of all, the complex reminds us that Black women are loveless and Black families endangered because sisters are

Sapphires—unsure of how to be properly submissive ladies who put their men first.

As (gasp) an actual married Black woman, I understand Erica's frustration. The popular mythology about Black women and marriage not only erases women like me, it burdens Black women alone with the health of Black relationships, it suggests that they need to make fundamental changes to who they are to attract partners, it assumes that they all want to marry (and marry men), and it suggests that singleness is bad for women and society. All those screaming headlines, condescending sermons, and self-help books are not, contrary to claims, about the endangered traditional African American family or the unique situations of Black women. They are simply the modern incarnation of long-held sexist and racist views that have plagued Black women for centuries.

· ·

Moments in Alright

In 2018, there were 2.4 million Black woman-owned businesses in America—up 164 percent from 2007.[3] That's almost three times the growth rate of women-owned businesses in general.

· ·

One legacy of the Moynihan Report is that Black American relationships are perpetually viewed as dysfunctional because of the number of nontraditional households led by single Black women. Of course, as of 2011, barely half of all US adults were married—a record low.[4] New marriages are declining in favor of cohabitation, single-person households, and single parenthood. This same shift is occurring around the globe. But African

American cohabitation, single-person households, and single parenthood are viewed as unique evidence of Black America's enduring retardation.

"Crazy" Single Ladies

In addition, Black men are just as single as their female counterparts. A *U.S. News & World Report* article on American households revealed that in 1990, 43 percent of Black men had never been married. In 2019, it was 51 percent. During that period, the percentage of Black women who were unmarried increased from 37 to 47 percent.[5] If discussion of the marriage crisis were driven simply by concern that the Black community has access to the societal and economic benefits of matrimony, then surely time devoted to dissecting the problems of unmarried Black men would equal talk about unmarried Black women. But that simply isn't how things work. Single men are not viewed as broken and ripe for lessons in what women want. It is single women who are considered societal problems.

Once, at the ripe old age of twenty-two, I was at a party, when a guy began (clumsily) chatting me up:

"So, do you have a boyfriend?" he asked.

"No," I replied.

"Oh, what's wrong with you, then?"

"Sorry?" I said, puzzled.

"I mean, dudes should be interested in a woman like you. If you don't have a boyfriend, something must be wrong. You must be one of those crazy women."

If madness is the mark of female singleness, the delirium is spreading. The percentage of married women across all races is decreasing.[6] Despite this shift, society's views on women and marriage have hardly changed since the Irish essayist George Bernard Shaw wrote, at the start of the twentieth century: "It is a woman's business to get married as soon as possible, and a man's to keep unmarried as long as possible."[7] Singleness and its associated freedoms are viewed as a man's game. And a woman without a wedding band, or at the very least an adoring male partner to signal her worthiness, is to be viewed as warily as a steak without a USDA stamp—something must be rotten there.

It is as it ever was. Way back in the seventeenth century, never-married women of a certain age were called "thornbacks," on the assumption that they were hardened creatures like the spiny-tailed thornback fish.[8] An article written by Kate Constance in the September 25, 1957, *Kansas City Star* is emphatic: "If you are 30 years old and aren't married, something is wrong. Very likely it is you—your attitudes, your personality, your objectives or your appearance."[9] There have been more dire historical outcomes for single women: a disproportionate number of the 344 people accused of witchcraft in colonial New England were single women.[10] We can, I suppose, take heart that today's single women aren't being burned at the stake. Women—be they citizens of colonial Salem or modern-day St. Louis—are judged and valued based on their ability to attract and please men above much else. An unchosen woman is likely not responding to the universal needs and desires of men. And men's desires are *always* reasonable, no matter the personal cost to the women who must meet them. Women, on the other hand, should expect little.

Ladies and Beasts of Burden

So, when talk turns to Black marriage, the rub seems not that Black people aren't getting married, but that Black *women* are not. And it is impossible not to recognize the prejudice behind the insistence that Black single women need to be taught (interestingly, often by men) how to be good wives and women. Because the conversation about Black marriage positions Black women as the cause of the problem, it is Black women who are expected to sacrifice for the greater good. *The New Yorker* illustrates this in a 2003 article titled "The Marriage Cure," which profiles Black women attending a church-led marriage advocacy program: "[It is] an unhappy but unavoidable fact that women are this social policy's beasts of burden."[11] Any effort to uplift a community that requires half its members be consigned to beast-of-burden status deserves to be met with skepticism, but that idea is as pervasive in the pulpit of the neighborhood African Methodist Episcopal (AME) church and the corner barbershop as it is on CNN.

The conversation about Black marriage particularly admonishes educated and successful Black women for their competence. Comedian-turned-relationship-expert Steve Harvey says in his bestselling book *Act like a Lady, Think like a Man*: "If you've got your own money, your own car, your own house, a Brinks alarm system, a pistol and a guard dog, you're probably shouting from the rooftops that you don't need a man to provide for you or protect you, then we'll see no need to keep coming around."[12]

Reprimanding women for, as Harvey says, "being the masters of 'handling it,'" robs us of our accomplishments while convincing vulnerable men that their manhood is dependent on the weakness of women.[13] This is particularly damaging in the Black community, which faces an even broader achievement gap between men and women than do other races. (For instance, women make up 66 percent of African Americans completing bachelor's degrees and 71 percent of those completing master's degrees.) Forcing Black women to justify their success to partners, who should be their biggest cheerleaders, is a troubling message for both Black women and men.

Carolyn Edgar's ex-husband told her that her achievements— a Harvard Law degree, a partnership, and a six-figure salary— made him feel like less of a man. And he attempted to bolster his manhood through verbal, emotional, and physical abuse.[14]

"He was pretty candid about it," Carolyn, fifty-five, says. "In his first marriage, he was the breadwinner and he liked that. Of course, I could have quit and we could have lived off of his paycheck, but he enjoyed the perks that came with my salary."

Her husband was eager to control the family finances, and Carolyn tried to alleviate his feelings of inadequacy by acquiescing to purchases that she knew were impractical and unwise. He chafed at her attempts to be frugal but resented the source of the money that paid for fancy cars and her three-carat engagement ring. He accused her of being both controlling and too meek. "'It's hard to believe you went to Harvard, the way you let people run all over you.'" He called her a whore and also too fat to be desirable.

"I would fight back and lash out, but it was killing me," Carolyn says. "I was drowning my sorrow in food and alcohol. I came to the realization that I would not survive if I stayed married. I knew I would kill myself."

The final straw came when she finally unburdened herself to her mother, who had survived an abusive marriage to Carolyn's father. "She said, 'That sounds just like my marriage.' That's the day I knew I had to leave, because I could see years down the line, my daughter calling me crying about her marriage and me saying the same thing. I had to get out.

"Marriage, when it works, is amazing. I like men. I like companionship. I like all the great things that go along with having a partner," Carolyn says. "I sometimes find myself longing for that connection with another person. But I've realized it's not worth it to sacrifice the other things that are important to me just to have a man around."

Real (Complicated) Love

The action plan being sold to Black women is not one likely to result in a love based on friendship, mutual respect, and common ground. How can a Black woman find someone to love her just as she is if she is constantly encouraged to be someone else— to execute some rote and reductive performance to appeal to the alleged universal needs of the opposite sex?

Speaking of men, the narrative around Black marriage generally supposes that men are the only people Black women can partner with. When I wrote the first edition of *Sisters*, gay marriage was not yet legal. And outside of the LGBTQ community, people talked much less about the myriad ways one can commit romantically or express gender. But no matter what the state or straight communities have said, Black women have always had loving, sustaining romantic relationships with other women. To leave queer Black women out of discussions of marriage is to overlook a significant Black woman identity—one that has underpinned the notion of liberated coupling, as well as the movement for Black women's liberation in the bodies of women like Audre Lorde, Alice Walker, Pauli Murray, and the Combahee River Collective.

"The lesbian—that woman who, as Judy Grahn says, 'has taken a woman lover'—has succeeded in resisting the slave master's imperialism in that one sphere of her life. The lesbian has decolonized her body. She has rejected a life of servitude implicit in Western, heterosexual relationships and has accepted the potential of mutuality in a lesbian relationship—roles notwithstanding," feminist activist Dr. Cheryl Clarke wrote in her seminal essay, "Lesbianism as Resistance."[15]

Whether queer or straight, the happily married women I interviewed for this book say that they resolutely approached relationships as complicated, whole women, not narrower, quieter versions of themselves. Their unions came not through playing games or following rules but by forming unique and intimate connections with the right partner. And they maintain that their marriages are stronger for it.

Nichelle Hayes, who has been married for thirty-one years, says, "I cringe at the idea of being chosen. It's like you're sitting on a shelf waiting for someone to come by and pick you up instead of meeting someone and having a connection and the two of you saying, 'I think this works for us.'

"I found someone who I thought—and still think—is a good person that I could build a life with. He is a good father and provider. He has integrity and is loyal. He has worked hard and he's been there. He cares for me deeply. It was a good choice."[16]

Yes, married Black women do exist, contrary to popular wisdom. In fact, most Black women over thirty-five have been married.[17] (This was surprising news to many of the single Black women I spoke to, so indoctrinated are they by the idea that Black women don't marry.)

"I primarily define myself as married, but I need to talk about why . . . why I as a feminist define myself that way," says D. Henry.[18] "My husband had cancer. I have a deep sense of what it means to put my relationship first. Things were so precarious for us. . . . [A wife] is not all that I am. [But when asked to define myself,] it is one of the first things I would say. I identify as a storyteller. I identify as a feminist. I identify as a nerd. I identify as a political junkie. But he comes first, because I love him best."

In 2009, D.'s husband, John, had his appendix removed after experiencing back pain. The extracted organ didn't look healthy. A biopsy revealed a very rare and aggressive form of cancer. The next several months were filled with chemotherapy, a nasty infection that gave John blind spots and forced doctors to discontinue his treatment regimen, and worry.

Her husband, D. says, is not a noble sufferer. "He didn't handle it well. There was a lot of taking things out on me. And I wasn't dealing with it well. There was the nastiness, where I was screaming at him in his hospital bed and then running out to the parking garage to cry over what a shitty person I was for screaming at him in his hospital bed. Lather. Rinse. Repeat. I couldn't even get the dog to function normally. The whole house just came screeching to a very angry halt."

D. and John went to see a marriage counselor, who said, "I like you guys. You're going to be easy. You love each other. You're just fighting because of the cancer."

"We came out of that willing to explicitly define who we intend to be to each other. Who we want to be and what we need from each other. We came out with just a strong, strong marriage.

"As I watched him get better and get stronger and become more himself again, we also got to become *ourselves* again. And I got to forgive myself for not being the angel, martyr wife I somehow thought I had to be. We came out of it seasoned. We loved each other a lot, but we were untested. On the other side of it, we know we can do anything. And that's an amazing thing to have. I love him more now than before."

In her early twenties, D. could hardly have guessed she would wind up here—in her seventh year of marriage and awaiting her first child. She didn't know what she wanted to do with her life—use her theater degree, write a book, move to California or abroad—but it didn't entail staying in one place.

Marriage is not a happy tradition in D.'s family. Most of her aunts, uncles, and cousins remain single. Her maternal grandparents, though mellowed in recent years, were once quite different. "There was definitely a lot of sniping and occasional projectiles." Her parents' marriage was disastrous.

Being in a loving marriage has required D. to do a lot of internal work, "learning how to trust and how to argue . . . learning how to rely on someone and be okay with relying on someone. I still feel a twinge here and there when I thought something was going to get done and it didn't. I have to realize that sometimes people just dawdle. It doesn't mean they are unreliable."

D. met John when he walked into the place where she tended bar. In short order, she fell "sideways stupid" in love with this good, loyal man who "wakes up every morning and the whole world is new. He can fix things. He can talk to you about philosophy and rewire the house. And he has yummy broad shoulders."

And he gets her.

"From the moment we got together, it was perfect. We were very much in the same place. We have a lot in common—a similar mindset and way of thinking." Recalling the word games the couple likes to play, D. adds, "The nerds inside us speak to each other."

This union, D. says, is more kismet than any right combination of tactics undertaken to escape singleness.

"My cousins who are unmarried are much prettier than I am and much kinder to strangers. A few of them could be perfectly good candidates for sainthood. It's not about that. It's really about time and place. But you can't sell luck. Nobody's going to buy luck. People want to buy an action plan.

* *

Moments in Alright

In 2008 and 2012, Black women led the United States in voter turnout. They also played a significant role in turning Virginia "blue" in 2013, leading that state's voters in turnout for the gubernatorial election—signaling hope for future elections.[19]

* *

"If I had never met him and I hadn't gotten married, I would have been okay. If I had met him and it hadn't worked out, that wouldn't be okay. I never cared about being married. I care about being married to John. I don't know that I'm a very good wife. I know that I'm a very good wife for him."

D. doesn't fit the popular narrative of Black womanhood not only because she is married, but also because her partner is a non-Black man. The freak-out over low Black marriage rates is connected to fears about the disappearance of Black families. And women, more so than men, are conditioned to be the keepers of family and culture. Black women viewed to be abdicating that responsibility are thought to be selling out in a way that men (who, when they date outside the race, get their own share of grief) are not. Hooking up with "the (White) man" is viewed as dancing with the Devil. And loving a non-Black man of color is reduced to perversion or fetish. (Overheard by a Black woman walking with her Latino husband: "Well, I guess that Chinaman is hung if she's with him.") It's no wonder that only 12 percent of Black women marry interracially.[20]

The idea that Black women should expand our racial romantic horizons has gained ground. The idea was the thesis of Ralph Richard Banks's 2012 book *Is Marriage for White People?* Black women should be free to partner with whomever they choose, but the idea that non-Black men are itching to marry Black women has a flaw. Black women occupy a specific and not enviable place in the romantic hierarchy. Centuries of stereotyping have done them no favors. Research has shown that in the increasingly popular world of online dating, Black women get less love than any other group of women.[21] Even Black men are less likely to respond to their online profiles. As one interviewee told me, "Everyone keeps telling Black women that we should be open to dating different types of men, but no one is telling men to be more open to dating us."

When Tiffany Met Trayvia

"You know I can't marry a woman. Right?"[22]

Tiffany Allen, thirty-four, was raised a Baptist, and her religious upbringing had taught her that loving another woman was immoral. And, for most of her life, her government said that marrying another woman was illegal. Now she struggled to believe that building a life with another woman was okay.

"If it was right, then [I] should be able to get married and [I couldn't]."

So she hatched a plan to maybe get what her heart wanted, while technically doing what "good" Black Christian women do— marry a man.

"I had a gay guy friend. I used to daydream that he and I would get married and then whoever we loved would marry each other," Tiffany says. "We would just live in condos next door to each other. And we would just be like best friend couples. And we would know—the four of us—that the two girls were together and the two guys were together, but the rest of the world . . ."

So when Tiffany met Trayvia White, she wanted to be clear: "You know I can't marry a woman. Right?"

The women were both volunteering, helping the residents of a neighborhood apartment complex that had caught fire. Tiffany was doing her Olivia Pope thing. She is a fixer. A doer. A planner. A take-charge person. Trayvia noticed her.

"It was her voice," Trayvia, thirty-one, says. "She has this rasp, and I love that. I went home that day and told my ex, 'I met a really cool girl. I've been saying I need more friends. I think she'd be a great friend.'"

They were friends—at first—taking endless trips to Target together and FaceTiming at night. After four months, they moved in together.

Tiffany laughs. "Lesbian years are different than other human years . . . In our world, a day is like a week, a week is like a month, a month is like a year. Okay?"

And with Trayvia, it seemed untenable for Tiffany to pretend.

Not with Trayvia, who nurtures her. "She's really good at that, which is weird for me. I've never really been in that relationship. I've always been the fixer. I've never had a person to do things for me, except my mommy."

Not with Trayvia, who came out at seventeen and had to leave her mother's house because of it. Trayvia, who had to fight so fucking hard for her first relationship that lasted nine years, during which she raised a whole kid. Trayvia knew, even as a girl, that she would marry a woman. "My father married my stepmom when I was nine," she says. "The things that my father did, I was like, 'I can't wait to treat my wife that way.' I never saw what my father did as something to look for in a man. I've always felt it was interesting how he was, and I couldn't wait to be that for my wife."

There is no reason to hide with Trayvia, who loves Tiffany's full self—the one that she tried so hard to hide from previous partners.

"'Cause I'm extra," Tiffany says. "I sing random songs and dance to commercials and make up songs about picking my toenails. I do whatever it is because it just happens to pop in my head. And I will be sitting in silence and randomly laughing. Or say something offensive and then be like, 'Oh crap. That shouldn't be said out loud.'

"But I can do that with her. I don't have to censor myself. I don't have to be perfect. I don't have to have it all together. And I have someone to do that or not do it with for the rest of my life. And that's just magical."

Not with Trayvia, who was strong in what she needed from a partner: "I wanted to make sure that this was something that [Tiffany] wanted; it wasn't just, 'Oh, I love you! And I want to be with you, so I want to try this.' I didn't want that. That is wrong to me. That's morally wrong. If this is something that we were going to do, I will be there for you 110 percent. But I need to know that this is something that you want. I'll be in your life regardless."

Tiffany fell in love with Trayvia and thought, "'Oh, hell!' I was sitting in the therapist's office. And I was like, 'Why am I in love with a woman? Dammit! I wasn't supposed to fall in love with her. This was not the plan!'

"But I can't be with her and not want to give everything that I am to her. And I can't hide something that is the most important part of my life . . . for the rest of my life."

Real love demands authenticity.

Trayvia says, "There's nothing that you can accomplish in an intimate relationship if you do not deal with those things that fucked you up. You have to be able to unravel yourself. If you cannot unravel yourself with yourself, you can't unravel yourself with someone else.

"I feel the definition of a relationship or a successful relationship is so warped nowadays. Instead of being our authentic selves. We have decided to become other people so that we can make other people happy. Everyone is fighting to not heal."

After three years, Tiffany and Trayvia got married—on October 10, 2020, in the middle of a pandemic. Tiffany thought, "10/10/2020 would be so cute. And [Trayvia] was like, 'That's cool.'" And Tiffany did her fixer thing and got a minister.

Trayvia says, "I like the security of [marriage]. I feel like I can move forward in my life in ways that you really can't when you're just dating or in a relationship with somebody. My whole life . . . I just didn't feel like I had a solid foundation. Choosing to be married to Tiffany has allowed me to move forward in every aspect of my life . . . having a partner . . . [I] have that support, that's right next to [me]."

The Allen-Whites have a ritual before they go to sleep each night. They lie together and talk about politics and memes and the day. And they say "I love you." Tiffany insists that it is all delightfully mushy.

Society's insistence that Black women mold themselves to someone else's whims and desires, simply to be married, means too many of them miss out on deep, authentic, sustaining love—love that requires you to heal yourself and show up fully and to insist on a partner who does the same. And love is the thing, not a marriage license. Unfettered love is the revolution.

"We are two women who love each other and we make that decision to love each other every single day," Trayvia says. "Don't try to define your relationship based off someone else's expectations. Your marriage or relationship, your commitment, is uniquely yours and gets to be designed by you."

Single and Loving It

Erica Johnson, who I introduced at the opening of this chapter, admits that marriage was never a wise fit for her.

"My mom says she remembers me coming up to her when I was five and saying, 'I'm never getting married, and I'm never having children.' I knew that there were things that I wanted to do in my life. I felt like marriage would get in the way of that. Turns out that ended up being true. I ended up getting married. It did get in the way of the things that I wanted to do. I probably should have listened to myself a little bit more."

Today, she is content and open to commitment, even if she doesn't plan to marry again. Erica says she has all the things that eluded her as a married woman. "It's my space. It's my mess. Life is pretty good, despite the challenges, despite the financial stuff, despite the health stuff. Life is really, really good right now. I've got this. Who I am, she's flawed. She's not perfect. Not that anybody needs to be perfect anyway. She is a really, really cool person. She'd be a great person to get to know. She's got a lot to offer."

The fearmongering over single Black woman does *all* women a disservice because it fails to acknowledge that women who are single—whether by choice or fate—can and do have happy and successful lives. Most married women interviewed for this book speak of their single days fondly, not as some penance they've thankfully escaped. Men are not the only sowers of oats. Singleness for women can be liberating and fun and can offer limitless opportunities, especially today, when the number of single households in America exceeds married ones. In a 2007 article in *USA Today*, Pat Palmieri, author and social historian at Teachers College at Columbia University, writes: "It's probably the best moment for singles in our history . . . because of the attitudes of popular support and the numbers."[23]

At forty, Kim Akins, then a single attorney, didn't see herself getting married, but it's not that she was closed to the idea. In her twenties, she came close, but it never seemed the right time.[24]

"I wanted to experience the world on my own. When I first considered getting married, I remember thinking that I hadn't seen enough of the world. I thought, 'I need to fall on my face by myself first before I become dependent on somebody else.'"

And then, after a certain age, she figured it wouldn't happen. But, Akins says, her life was good. She threw a party to celebrate that. She reckoned, why should she have to say "I do" to be feted by friends and family? She vowed to "live like a rich man," with no regrets. She traveled. She partied. She lived well. And she treated her friends to pictures of strippers and boy toys—one known only as "Peach," for his taut and rounded rear.

Akins says, "I am one of a few of my friends that claim feminism. They perceived me as acting 'wild.' I saw them as lacking the courage to live by their own rules."

Even her online dating profile was geared more toward fun than commitment. She noted a preference for long-distance arrangements. But love and commitment hit her by surprise, when what was intended as a casual online dalliance with a musician living hundreds of miles away turned into something deeper. After exchanging lengthy emails and talking on the phone for hours every night, the couple had a first date in Las Vegas.

"When we parted, it was like a scene from *Casablanca*. I was in hysterics. He looked at me and said, 'This is the beginning.'"

It was.

"I am very deliberate about my decisions," Kim says. "But marrying him was the easiest decision I ever made in my life."

Would she live her single life differently, though?

No.

"I would tell Black women to live their lives to the fullest. Don't wait for a partner to take you to the Alps. Go see them yourself. When you fill yourself up, you're more attractive, and if romance doesn't happen, you're still full of you."

Chapter 4

Motherhood
Between Mammy and a Hard Place

At the 2012 Democratic National Convention, First Lady Michelle Obama announced that her most important role in the White House is "mom-in-chief."[1]

Some White feminists weren't having it.

What was up with this Ivy League–trained, corporate legal powerhouse making like a political wifebot? As writer Libby Copeland lamented on *Slate* magazine's *Double X* blog, "Why are presidential candidates' wives all the same?"[2]

Except Michelle LaVaughn Robinson Obama, from the South Side of Chicago, ain't Laura Bush. Or even Hillary Clinton. (There is evidence First Lady 45 Melania Trump may want to be Michelle Obama. But I digress.) Michelle Obama is a Black woman. And her ability to prioritize motherhood—much less be the symbol of motherhood for a nation—was revolutionary.

Black women are not the inheritors of the cult of true womanhood's picture of wifely domesticity. For them, the fight has not been to prove that they can be something other than mothers as much as it has been to have the myriad ways they mother recognized and cherished in a society whose family values rarely include them and those they love.

It has always been accepted that Black women can care for other people's children. In slavery, many of them did the dirty work of homemaking—the cooking, cleaning, and mommying for masters and mistresses. Later, Black domestics helped make it possible for middle-class White women to enter a workforce of which Black women (and poor women of all races) were already an exploited part. In 2014, the number of "Black women pushing White babies around" on the Upper West Side of New York City prompted a photography exhibition by Ellen Jacobs called *Substitutes*.[3] But modern Black mothers exist between this comfortable evocation of Mammy and a hard place.

· ·

Moments in Alright

Noreen Raines became a self-proclaimed "science nerd" after receiving a microscope for Christmas when she was eight years old. In 2005, Raines, the mother of four, launched Big Thinkers to inspire lifelong science learning in the state of Georgia, through interactive stage shows, in-school programming, birthday parties, summer camps, and workshops.[4]

· ·

Do Black Mothers Matter?

Serena Williams knew something was wrong. A pulmonary embolism had nearly killed her in 2011 and she was prone to the condition. When she began having difficulty breathing after delivering her daughter Olympia in 2017, Williams alerted a nurse to the danger.

"I need a CT scan and a heparin drip."[5]

The medical team at the hospital was unconvinced; pain medication must have left Williams confused, they decided. They tried several other interventions before listening to the new mother. A CT scan eventually revealed several life-threatening blood clots in her lungs. By then, the embolism had triggered coughing that ruptured Williams' cesarean section incision. During surgery to close it, doctors found a large hematoma, which required yet more surgery. Williams spent the first six weeks of little Olympia's life bedridden. The tennis legend's story could have had a tragic end.

Black motherhood attracts none of the gauzy sanctity afforded White mothers. Never is a White woman viewed as more fragile and worthy of protection as when she is carrying White life. Meanwhile, Black women are treated like livestock, requiring little care for what is surely just biological imperative to breed more valueless offspring. They are not protected from the toxic psychological stress of systemic racism or an indifferent medical system. As a result, Black women are three to four times more likely to die from pregnancy-related causes as White women, and their babies more than twice as likely to die as White ones.[6] And this is not solely a problem of class and access; even millionaire, twenty-three-time Grand Slam champions are at risk.

Because Black women's ability to conceive and bring forth new life is not cherished or valued, they often receive medical care that fails to take their fertility and childbearing into account. Because Black femme humanity goes unrecognized, they face medical practitioners who ignore their pain and discomfort. If society does not believe Black lives matter, how then can Black life-bringers matter?

"I am now an exhibit in Ripley's Believe It or Not," Jamie Nesbitt Golden remembers thinking, as she lay splayed on an examination table while a succession of doctors gawked at the uterine fibroid that was leeching nutrients from her baby.[7]

"It's like an *SNL* sketch, because the doctor's like, 'Wow! This is big! This is the big fibroid. Jim, have you seen this?'

"When I look up, maybe three or four people are in this exam room looking at my hoohah and the big-ass fibroid. I'm in my early thirties and I'm not as vocal as I am now. I'm scared shitless by this entire process. I am mortified that this is happening, but I don't feel comfortable advocating for myself."

Black women are more likely than White women to have fibroids, which are noncancerous uterine tumors, and to suffer from complications, including infertility and the inability to carry a healthy pregnancy.[8] There are less invasive treatments, but a Black woman is at least twice as likely as a White woman to have her uterus removed through hysterectomy—often during childbearing years. Jamie had been assured years ago that her fibroid would not cause problems; now it had made her pregnancy high risk.

This had been Jamie's worst fear. A journalist, she knew about the risks of being a pregnant Black woman: "I'm the girl who is Googling maternal death stats at midnight." She had heard her friends' harrowing stories. Plus, Jamie had already suffered one miscarriage, and the indifference of the attending physician still haunted her.

She would have to spend her second trimester on bed rest, rising for appointments with a high-risk specialist whose crowded office in the birthing center left many of his mostly Black pregnant patients sitting on the floor. It was no better in the exam room, where Jamie says the specialist was dismissive. "They assume you're Black, poor and you don't know what you're talking about."

Doctors induced Jamie's labor when her amniotic fluid levels dropped. She remembers waiting for her husband to arrive at the hospital, watching the monitors that showed her baby's heart rate. She had hoped for a supportive, nurturing, and natural birthing experience. Instead, "suddenly I'm high. The one doctor I do trust—[a Black woman]—is on vacation; they have to call her. I'm waiting and holding my breath because I don't want to do this without her," Jamie remembers. "Next thing, I'm getting wheeled into the operating room. They have you hooked up to these machines. You're hearing your heart rate drop. And it's like, 'Is something [bad] happening to me?' I'm sort of freaking out. My husband's holding my hand and he sees everything. His eyes are growing wide as saucers; he looks like he's about to faint because they've ripped me open and they're sort of rummaging through like I'm grandma's purse. No one is explaining anything to us or talking to us."

Jamie labored for six hours. "I don't know how women do this for longer." She delivered a beautiful baby boy—Langston. Less than forty-eight hours later, she was home, held together by metal staples and still struggling to breastfeed. (The lactation specialist had been perfunctory and impatient.) The first year would be hard for the new mother. After three days home,

Jamie's temperature spiked. She had developed an infection in her C-section incision that sent her back to the hospital. (Black women are more likely to have complications like this.)

And then there was the postpartum depression. As a Black woman, Jamie struggled to find a mental health professional who was both supportive and culturally competent. One non-Black therapist violated Jamie's privacy and also warned her against taking evening walks around her Hyde Park, Chicago, neighborhood to reduce stress. "You'll get raped!"

Her marriage began to fray. She wanted to return to work but could not. She stopped caring for herself. She felt isolated when her husband returned to work. These situations are not uncommon for new mothers. But for Black women they are amplified and made worse by societal indifference driven by racism and stereotype. Strong women don't have vulnerabilities. Beasts navigate gestation and childbirth alone. Mammies nurture naturally. And a society that hates Black people does not care to abet bringing new ones into the world.

Jamie loves her son, now eleven, to the moon and back. He is named for the brilliant Black poet Langston Hughes. She is enraptured by the way he learns new things. "When he learns something new, he's so excited about it and he's so ready to share it. And it just, it just melts you." But she is firm that, after her experience, she did not want to have another baby. (She cannot, now, because her fibroid did eventually lead to the removal of her uterus.)

"Every time I read a story about a Black woman dying in labor, I go back to that place where I was a decade ago," Jamie says. "This isn't how it should be. None of us should be dying from giving birth in supposedly the most technologically advanced country in the world. I hope that things will get better. I hope that people are taking these stories and this data and are trying to truly make change [for Black mothers]. But I also know we live in a society that loves to devalue [Black women]—that loves to keep [its] foot on our necks."

Attack of the Single Black Mother

Nearly 70 percent of Black births happen outside marriage.[9] From conservative political candidates to Black clergy, folks will tell you that statistic is a sin and a shame. For a society that is mistrustful of sexually active, unmarried women and wedded to the superiority of male-led households, those numbers demonstrate unchecked aberrance and are used to confirm stereotypes about Black women's femininity and sexuality. This statistic is positioned as the reason for every social ill plaguing the Black community and, once again, very likely the fault of Black women.

In 2013, conservative columnist George Will said on ABC's *This Week* that single mothers are "the biggest impediment" to Black progress—bigger even than the loss of voting rights.[10] (Stacey Abrams, no doubt, would like a word.) Jimi Izrael, then a frequent contributor to NPR, wrote in his 2010 book *The Denzel Principle* that high rates of Black divorce and single-parent families "really reflects less on Black men and more on Black women and their inability to make good choices."[11]

Dr. Sarah Jackson says that Black women's sexuality and motherhood have been part of public discourse since slavery, when our reproduction was an integral part of the economy, like the livestock that kept the agricultural engine going.[12] People were as inclined to talk about Black women birthing babies as they were cows bearing calves. And, like those cows, Black women were viewed as uncivilized and unintentional breeders.

The institution of slavery required a voluntary blindness to the idea of Black family. No doubt this history influences the medical care (or lack thereof) Black women receive when pregnant, as well as how they are viewed as mothers. "If you're treating a group of people like animals, you have to believe that they're not capable of making the same emotional bonds with their children that you are. Otherwise, you might feel bad about selling their children off down the river," Jackson says.

Here again, the Moynihan Report and its support for the stereotypes of the Matriarch, Sapphire, and Jezebel play a role in ensuring that the public discussion of Black motherhood is relentlessly negative.

"If the male isn't the primary breadwinner of the family, then the children of that family are forever deviant. It's right there on the page," says Jackson.

Ronald Reagan, in his 1976 presidential campaign, abetted this idea with his bogeywoman, the "welfare queen."[13] His frequently repeated anecdote about the Cadillac-driving Chicago woman who swindled government programs out of hundreds of thousands of dollars by using disguises, fake names and addresses, and possibly a stolen baby cemented the idea that Black female reproduction is unreasonable, is tied to lasciviousness, and reflects a desire to leech off the state rather than to be a loving parent and contributor to the future of society.[14]

The structure of the American family is undeniably changing. Just before the first edition of this book was released, the US Supreme Court legalized gay marriage in all fifty states, opening the door for a new picture of family.[15] But overall, US marriage rates hit an all-time low in 2020.[16] Cohabitation is on the rise.[17] Women are having fewer babies and having them later.[18] Nearly 40 percent of all American births happen outside of marriage.[19]

And women are more likely to be primary breadwinners than in the past.[20] According to a 2015 Pew Research Center report, two-parent households are declining and "there is no longer one dominant family form in the U.S."[21]

But Black women and their families are still seen as dysfunctional, and uncommonly so.

Opponents of single motherhood say they have Black children's best interests in mind and point to decades of research that indicates that children do best when they're raised in healthy two-parent families. But, according to the Center for Law and Social Policy, research results related to the offspring of single-parent households are often oversimplified and exaggerated.[22] Most children in single-parent families grow up just fine, and it is still unclear how much of the disadvantages to children are caused by poverty or family structure or whether marriage itself makes the difference or the type of people who commonly marry.

Demonizing single Black motherhood does not improve the lives of children. On the contrary, the idea that 70 percent of Black boys and girls are congenitally damaged stigmatizes them.

"It's messed up that we have to figure out how to keep our kids from being negatively impacted by generations of misinformation about the way that our households are run," says Stacia Brown, thirty-five.[23] "I don't want my child to feel that the way we live is something that we have to defend to the world."

Stacia herself was raised by a single mother. And she learned from her mother to protect her own daughter from the stain of so-called illegitimacy.

"We didn't use stigmatized language around our family structure when I was growing up," she says.

And when a young Stacia was confronted with condemning language about her family, it felt foreign. "I thought, 'We're happy here.' It didn't feel like, 'Oh my gosh, I don't have a dad and my life is definitely really bad because of this.' I mean, I do have a daddy, he just lived in another state. I have a lot of things that felt like bigger barriers to my long-term success than fatherlessness or whatever."

Stacia, who co-parents with her child's father, says, "We need to, in our households, set our standard for how we're going to feel about ourselves. When your kids hear you say, 'I don't want to be a statistic,' they feel like their household is . . . there's something wrong with it. You're bringing that into your house.

"Even if somebody at school dogs them about it, when they come home, you've got to be able to say, 'Nah, we're not accepting that.'"

The negative focus on single Black motherhood is also not about helping Black communities. If it were, those who rail against unmarried mothers would spend at least equal time calling for affordable family planning and reproductive health care, universal access to good childcare, improved urban school systems, a higher minimum wage, and college education that doesn't break the banks of average people. They would admit that the welfare-queen image is a distortion and a distraction from addressing unrelenting systemic racism and White supremacy that has worn on Black families for centuries.

America is a place where one in a thousand Black men and boys can be expected to be killed by police in their lifetime and Flint, Michigan, officials infamously exposed nearly one hundred thousand mostly Black residents, including children, to lead-tainted water for more than a year.[24] But the plight of the African American community can allegedly be blamed mostly on the moral failings of Black women who do not marry the fathers of their children—no matter how hard those mothers work to build good lives for their families. Even the Queen of Soul is not immune from the stigma of single Black motherhood. A Georgia pastor chose the occasion of Aretha Franklin's 2018 funeral to castigate single mothers like the activist and eighteen-time Grammy Award winner, who raised four boys. In his remarks "honoring" Franklin, Rev. Jasper Williams Jr. called raising a child without a father in the home "abortion after birth" and insisted that a woman cannot raise a boy to manhood.[25]

Heidi Renée Lewis, forty, says condemnation of single-parent families also unduly shames mothers trying to do their best. She tells a story about attending a neighborhood outing with her oldest son and his father while she was pregnant with their second child.[26]

"Our kids are only nineteen months apart. This one woman that I grew up with said to my cousin, 'Oh my God! I can't believe Heidi is having another baby. Didn't she just have a baby?' My cousin said, 'Well at least they're both by the same man!'"

Heidi's cousin had three children with two fathers. "She was kicking herself in the face to defend me," she says.

"I grew up with more examples of nontraditional than traditional. Women on welfare, struggling. All the women I knew on welfare worked, just like most people on welfare work. There was still this 'don't be like them' narrative. Why would I want to be like people who weren't being affirmed? People hate to feel ashamed."

Heidi's parents were married when she was born. They grew up together and were high school sweethearts. When they married, her father built a house for his young wife, across the street from his in-laws in a small Ohio town. But it was the eve of the 1980s crack epidemic, and Heidi's father became addicted. Her parents divorced.

Heidi always wanted to get married, in part to prove that she could do what her parents could not. A child of the '80s, she was partly influenced by popular culture—"[Whether the families were] piss poor like Roseanne and Dan or upper middle class like Clair and Cliff, we were being indoctrinated with that traditional family model"—but she was also guided by her beloved grandmother's conservatism. "My grandfather, even though he was a minister, was more forgiving than my grandmother. My grandmother was not for the shit like out-of-wedlock babies! Oh my God, no!

"What I really think I wanted was to have kids and for my kids to not have the family trouble that I had. They would not have to go through divorce, and they would not have to have a drug-addicted parent, and they would not have to have parents who married other people and made life uncomfortable that way."

In graduate school and unmarried (though in a committed relationship), Heidi became pregnant.

"I was devastated . . . not devastated, but I was scared. . . . I'll tell you how respectability crept its way back in. . . . I was like, 'Well, I'm not married, but at least I have a bachelor's degree! . . . I finished school, and I'm halfway through a master's. Damn! Can I get a break for that?'"

Heidi and her husband have been together for more than fifteen years. She often forgets exactly when they made it "official."

"I can't even remember. What is this, 2014? I think we got technically married in 2009? I don't know. Yeah, 2009. You know what? Our wedding anniversary is the same as the day we first got together. We didn't change the day 'cause we felt like we wanted to honor the whole eleven years. Who gives a shit that it's not on the official paper?"

If America were having an honest conversation about Black motherhood, the screeds about the scourge of baby mamas would also note that birth rates among African American women are lower than ever before in recorded history and that part of the explanation for the high percentage of out-of-wedlock Black babies lies with the fact that fewer Black women are marrying and many of those women are deciding not to have children. Married Black women are also having fewer children.[27]

No. The conversation about Black single motherhood in America is driven by gender- and race-biased moral panic and is primarily a means to exonerate systemic inequality for America's problems, while leveraging age-old stereotypes to scapegoat Black women and their children. The reduction of Black motherhood to concerns about indiscriminate fucking, emasculating Black men, draining the public teat, and releasing frightening, no-daddy-having offspring onto beleaguered American streets stains every Black mothering experience, no matter how much individual realities differ.

Despite their decades-long marriage, Michelle Obama was derisively called then-candidate Barack Obama's "baby mama" in a Fox News graphic.[28] Yvette Perry, a married mother of twins, found her swollen fingers uncomfortable in her wedding rings after giving birth. But she wore the rings anyway to avoid being stereotyped as a single Black mother. It didn't help. "A new graduate student in my program, who had seen me at a couple of welcome/orientation activities with my babies, kept going on about how much respect she had for me. It took me a while to figure out that she assumed I was a single mother."[29]

When life experiences collide with stereotypes, drawing a distinction can be even tougher, the burden heavier.

Forty-one-year-old Brandee Mimitzraiem is not the woman people imagine when they hear about single Black mothers.[30] She is working on her PhD in theology and philosophy and is a member of the clergy in the AME Church. She gave birth to two sons, becoming a single mother by choice after realizing at twenty-six that marriage would never be for her.

"I do see myself reflected a lot in the stereotype and it bothers me," she says. "You know, I've had to go on food stamps. My babies are on Medicaid right now, because I cannot afford insurance for the three of us.

"People say, 'You're getting a PhD. It's not the same. You're not like them.' But I am, and my kids go to school with 'them.' I take those issues of class very seriously. I'm not going to look down on somebody else because they don't have the same education as me. I don't have a baby daddy, but at the same time, I'm a Black single mom, whose kids are on Medicaid. And I get talked about horribly for actually raising my kids, too."

All Black mothers are forced to expend energy (as if being a parent isn't hard enough) trying to outrun the idea that they are bad mothers who birth and then neglect bad kids with uninvolved, bad daddies.

Now, *that* is a sin and a shame.

. . . .

Moments in Alright

Tanya Fields wants fellow mothers and children in her Bronx neighborhood to have access to locally sourced and nutritious food. She started the BLK ProjeK to create economic development opportunities for underserved women and is working to develop a women-led cooperative food business and urban farm using undeveloped land.[31]

. . . .

The Purposeful Mother

Most single Black mothers are not postgraduate-degree-holding pastors, but neither are they the pariahs of the public imagination. The negative perception of Black mothers flattens the experiences of single mothers and ignores single mothers by choice, single mothers whose partners are involved in their children's lives, unmarried mothers who live and parent with their partners, lesbian mothers, and married mothers in traditional families. It also obscures the fact that most Black mothers, no matter their family structure, attempt to thoughtfully and successfully raise their children.

"Black parenting is never theorized as something that has intentionality," says Heidi Renée Lewis. "It's like we're just . . . popping out babies."

But many single mothers take care to create strong support systems before their children enter the world—something that Brandee points out is important for traditional families, too. "Raising kids without a village is impossible. Period. If you're only dependent upon what's in your house to raise your children, your children are failing and you're failing as a parent."

Because Black mothers are positioned as "other," it is easy for people to miss the elements of universality in parenting experiences—the worrying, the work, and the joy.

Stacia says the things that keep her up at night have less to do with single mothering than mothering full stop. Her four-year-old suffers from hearing loss and has experienced some developmental delays. Stacia and her co-parent worry about how to best advocate for her. For four years, Stacia parented long distance with her child's father, who this year moved closer to be a bigger presence in his daughter's life, challenging the assumption that unless they are married, fathers always remain uninvolved.

The push and pull of co-parenting is not much different from what married parents do, Stacia says, pointing out that the burden of childcare is rarely shared equally even between married parents. There are negotiations over finances and quality time, whether one parent will stay home, how childcare will work, and who will fetch the children from school.

The commonalities of parenting are also apparent when Black mothers express their love for their children.

Brandee marvels at "how the world amazes them and the things that come out of their mouths." Stacia loves little girl hugs and affection and the new way being a mother makes her see the world, but also the mystery of conceiving and nurturing another human being.

Heidi says, "I get to teach my kids things. I get to make an impact on the world. I get to teach them values that I learned and also teach them things differently."

Brandi Summers becomes emotional while speaking about her baby daughter: "I didn't know I had the capacity to love anything as much as I love her. I couldn't draw or write how much I love her."[32]

It is clear that Black mothers are no different from other mothers in terms of their devotion and concern for their children. What is unique is how they are obligated to, from an early age, teach their children how to navigate their minority status and the racism that accompanies it.

"Being Black has demanded that I parent my children regarding race, gender, socioeconomic problems, and issues even when I wasn't ready, in the mood, whatever," says Heidi. "I did not ask to have to tell my daughter why she was the only brown girl in ballet. The world demanded that I do that, because she is just the kind of kid who picks up on that kind of shit.

"With the Trayvon Martin verdict, I had to tell my son that if you're in a situation where somebody is about to do something to you, don't just scream. Scream your address or your middle name or something to let somebody know who the hell you are. . . . I will never forget that fucking debate over who was screaming: George Zimmerman or Trayvon Martin. I said, 'Well, I got an answer for that! Scream some shit that nobody but you knows. Scream, 'Help me! This man is attacking me and my middle name is Aaron Patrick!'

"Why do I have to do that? Because I'm raising Black children in the United States of America in the twenty-first century."

* *

Moments in Alright

"My daughter sometimes slept under my desk when I worked nights," says DeShong Perry Smitherman, who became a mother at sixteen. DeShong went on to become an Emmy Award–winning news producer. And with her business partner, Ericka Gibson, she cofounded A Girl's Gift, Inc., a program designed to teach girls leadership and entrepreneurial skills.[33]

* *

Brandi says she has a lot of fears about "raising a Black girl in this world. My race still becomes very, very clear even in the fact that I'm a mom. I stopped noticing when I'm alone, like it's just me in a room full of White people, but if I'm with my daughter and we're in a room full of White people and White kids, I just notice it right away. I want her to be with some kids of color or I'm wondering what these parents are teaching their children about Black kids. I'm paranoid about all that. How is she going to see the world?"

But Black mothers find little support in addressing problems of race or the routine challenges (and joys) of parenting because the way people think about Black parenting is so limited.

Ain't I a Mommy?

In a 2008 *Bitch* magazine article titled "Ain't I a Mommy," Deesha Philyaw lamented the exclusion of Black mothers from the "mommy memoir" boom.[34] As a married Black stay-at-home mom, Philyaw found her experience virtually missing from parenting literature. Also, the stay-at-home mom versus working mom argument that the media seemed obligated to rehash ad nauseam was presented only through the eyes of upper-middle-class White women, ignoring that throughout the history of Black women in America, most of them have had no choice but to work.

"I really needed to see myself in those pages. In other memoirs, I saw college-educated, stay-at-home moms who felt equal parts gratitude, mental fatigue, and boredom, but I didn't see any women who were Black like me," Philyaw wrote.

Michelle Hughes, a single mother through adoption, says it is nearly impossible to find books about Black parents adopting Black children.[35]

"The only support you get is with other single Black-adoptive moms," she says. "I'm an organizer. If I don't have what I need, I put it together. I founded an African American adoption room because I couldn't find one on Facebook."

Stacia launched a blog called *Beyond Baby Mamas* "to talk about some of the feelings that I was having and the experiences and stigma and all that stuff like that, but then also some of the unique triumphs of being a co-parent or solo parent."

Many Black mothers find themselves having to create their own support systems online and elsewhere because the belief that all Black mothers are single and that single mothers are dysfunctional messes leaves the real needs of African American mothers unaddressed.

It is within this social context, with its poisoned view of Black motherhood, that our African American First Lady of the United States existed. Feminists that were eager to see Michelle Obama strike a blow against stereotyped roles for women should have known that she was doing just that. Far from commonplace, her presence as a mother in the White House defied conventions about Black women as mothers, wives, and caretakers for their families.

I imagine that a woman as accomplished as the former FLOTUS had the strength to make her needs known and that if she, for a time, chose motherhood, that was the role she wanted. That choice alone is a privilege not afforded most women in our modern economy, much less Black ones.

The pushback against the role Michelle Obama chose for herself is illustrative of the way Black mothers' needs, desires, and experiences are ignored in favor of the stories others would prefer to tell about them. It is no more noble to demand that a Black woman flex her Harvard Law degree instead of her role as a wife and mother than it is to insist that her family is illegitimate unless she is wearing a wedding ring. Just as it is devastating to ignore a Black mother's understanding of her body. All of these things are part of a sad history of acts against Black female agency and a case of public interference in Black women's private choices.

Those who wished to brand Michelle Obama a dangerous radical may have had it right—just not in the way they thought. My forever First Lady's most incendiary act of bomb throwing was when she stood on stage, the descendant of slaves, in front of millions, at an arena in what was once the Old South, and said unapologetically: "At the end of the day, my most important title is still 'mom-in-chief.' My daughters are still the heart of my heart and the center of my world."

Forget what you've heard. That proclamation was not business as usual. Many Black women, who struggle each day to have the glorious complexity of their motherhood noticed and valued, saw it for what it was—an act of rebellion.

And one not unlike the private resistance Black mothers across America enact daily, just by being.

"I didn't create the struggle. I didn't ask for these myths about the welfare queen and the mammy and the junk," Heidi says. "We're just trying to do as Black mothers the best we can with what we've been given, trying to be as radical as we can in a world that doesn't allow for radical anything to thrive.

"This is what I was born into, so I'm navigating that and trying to be true to whoever it is that I am, within that context, in the best way possible."

Chapter 5

Anger
Twist and Shout

What do you call a wildly successful writer, director, producer, and mother of three, who also happens to be a Black woman?

According to America's newspaper of record, you call her "angry."

Alessandra Stanley's *New York Times* review of ABC-TV's *How to Get Away with Murder* opened thusly: "When Shonda Rhimes writes her autobiography, it should be called 'How to Get Away with Being an Angry Black Woman.'"[1]

In the September 2014 article, Stanley praised Rhimes, the Midas touch behind the shows *Scandal* and *Grey's Anatomy*, for "doing more to reset the image of African-American women on television than anyone since Oprah Winfrey." She wrote:

> Her women are authority figures with sharp minds and potent libidos who are respected, even haughty members of the ruling elite, not maids or nurses or office workers.

Be it Kerry Washington on "Scandal" or Chandra Wilson on "Grey's Anatomy," they can and do get angry. One of the more volcanic meltdowns in soap opera history was Olivia's "Earn me" rant on "Scandal."

Ms. Rhimes has embraced the trite but persistent caricature of the Angry Black Woman, recast it in her own image, and made it enviable. She has almost single-handedly trampled a taboo even Michelle Obama couldn't break.

Her heroines are not at all like the bossy, sassy, salt-of-the-earth working-class women who have been scolding and uh-uh-ing on screen ever since Esther Rolle played Florida, the maid on "Maude."

Moments in Alright

Black women are less susceptible to internalizing sexist stereotypes about careers in STEM (science, technology, engineering, and math) than White women and show more interest in these rising fields.[2]

If Stanley's interpretation is to be believed, Shonda Rhimes is undeniably angry. She makes her Black female characters in her own image, and they, too, are angry. (It is unclear how Rhimes pours her Black lady anger into the many characters she creates who are not Black and not female.) But through some sleight of hand, she has been able to "get away with" presenting these angry Black women on TV. For instance, Stanley writes that Scandal's Olivia Pope is different from previous

Black female characters on television. She calls Florida Evans, of the 1970s sitcoms *Maude* and *Good Times*, "scolding" and "salt-of-the-earth working-class"—as if those descriptions fit together like peanut butter and jelly. And she dismisses *The Cosby Show*'s Clair Huxtable, who, incidentally, laid more truth-telling monologues on people than Florida and Olivia combined, as "benign and reassuring."

Small-Screen Sapphires

The *Amos 'n' Andy* show left the air in 1953, and yet folks still see Sapphire everywhere. Black women are believed to be quick to anger and even quicker to let you know it—always shouting with their faces twisted in a rictus of pique. And the ire of Black women is irrational and base—never justified. The idea that Black women are angry, hostile, and aggressive is pervasive and burdensome and leaves them vulnerable, unable to defend themselves when they need to.

Perhaps we should blame Mary-Ellis Bunim and Johnathan Murray, the producers who introduced *The Real World* on MTV in 1992, launching the heyday of reality TV and, with it, the golden age of the small-screen Sapphire.[3] Today, there are bad Black chicks all the time, up and down the dial. The angry Black woman is a reality-TV staple. In 2014, two popular reality shows ended with Black girl fisticuffs. On the *Real Housewives of Atlanta* (*RHOA*) reunion, a screeching Porsha Stewart catapulted herself on top of former Miss USA Kenya Moore.[4] And on *Love & Hip Hop Atlanta*, Joseline Hernandez took on all comers, punching faces and sending hair pieces askew. In the aftermath of the rumble, Hernandez assured viewers, "I come everywhere ready to fight."[5]

Stewart and Hernandez are just the latest in a long line of reality Sapphires, from Camille on season one of *America's Next Top Model*, through the reviled Omarosa Manigault-Stallworth on *The Apprentice*, to the overbearing NeNe Leakes on *RHOA*.

This reality, of course, is anything but. In her book *Reality Bites Back*, Jennifer L. Pozner writes, "This genre that calls itself 'unscripted' is carefully crafted to push all our culturally ingrained buttons. Offensiveness = hype = increased eyeballs for advertisers and cash for networks, making outrageous bigotry less a by-product of reality TV than its blueprint."[6]

It is not that reality producers have mostly angry Black women to choose from when casting the latest ode to consumerism and trifling behavior. It is that producers specifically search for, hire, and elevate those willing to traffic in gender, race, and class stereotypes in exchange for marginal fame. A mad Black woman aloft like a Valkyrie, weave flying and eyes ablaze, gets ratings and days of viral video and lights up social media like a Christmas tree. A calm and reasonable Black woman handling her life like a functional adult? Well, who wants to watch that?

As Manigault-Stallworth told *Time* magazine, "When I was a good girl, there were no cameras on. The minute I started arguing, there was a camera shooting me from every angle."[7]

She gave producers what they wanted, and they wanted the angry Black woman as spectacle and entertainment. The trope sells. Twelve million people watched the viral video "Sharkeshia" on the popular video-sharing site Worldstar Hip Hop. It showed a seventeen-year-old Black girl being confronted and brutally pummeled by her classmate Sharkeshia in a dispute over a boy.[8] Shock sites, like Worldstar Hip Hop, profit from violence by and against Black women. Like reality TV's Black female villains,

Worldstar's brawlers are leveraged to confirm the angry Black woman stereotype.

The proliferation of angry Black women in popular culture perhaps explains why so many Black women report that they are assumed to be angry by default.

First (Angry) Lady of the United States

"Generally speaking, I try hard to be happy and bubbly," says Gloria Pruitt, thirty-five.[9] "I recognize as a Black woman that I don't have the luxury of having a wide range of emotions for fear of being called angry. I'm careful about how I present myself, especially with non-Black people. Whenever you have a conversation with someone, you feel like you're carrying all of Black womanhood on your shoulders."

Even America's First Lady was supposedly angry. Since Barack Obama appeared on the national scene as a political figure, media and opponents have sought to paint his wife as an angrier, more radical, more aggressive, Blacker version of her husband—despite Michelle Obama being arguably more accessible and game than previous presidential spouses. She danced with Jimmy Fallon and mugged with basketball players, for God's sake. She was at least as pleasant and friendly as her predecessors.

Yet Alessandra Stanley, in her *New York Times* piece about Shonda Rhimes, joined the ranks of many who had accused the then FLOTUS of being angry. That smiling, friendly, sack-racing, double-Dutch jumping First Lady must have been a ruse to hide MObama's Sapphire within.

During the 2008 presidential campaign, a rumor spread of an explosive video of Michelle Obama giving a racially incendiary speech peppered liberally with the word "whitey."[10] As difficult as it should be to believe that a Harvard-educated executive and wife of a politician would give a presentation using a persona out of a Blaxploitation flick, the debunked conspiracy persists to this day.

As First Lady, Obama's every nonsmiling facial expression was analyzed and seen as a sign of persistent displeasure. A *New York Post* headline, following a memorial celebration for Nelson Mandela, crowed: "Michelle Not Amused by Obama's Memorial Selfie."[11] Below the headline was a slideshow of eleven images showing the president taking photos and joking with British Prime Minister David Cameron and Danish Prime Minister Helle Thorning-Schmidt, while Michelle Obama sits beside him, her face in repose. The accompanying article imagines the First Lady "grit[ting] her teeth in rage" and speaks of her "icy glare" and "angry looks." The *Post*'s response was a typical reaction as photos from the memorial went viral. The then FLOTUS was cast as the simmering harpy, eager to kill her husband's fun with a pretty, fun-loving White lady (Thorning-Schmidt). The mean Michelle buzz became so thick that the Agence France-Presse photographer responsible for the photo series came forward to assure the public that moments before the images were snapped, the First Lady had been laughing and joking with those around her.

You Know How Y'all Are

I asked Liz Hurston whether she has ever been pegged as an angry Black woman. "I had to think long and hard about this one," she said. "Not because there weren't enough examples, but because there were too many.[12]

"This has affected me since birth, especially growing up in a religious household. My father, due to the pain of his own upbringing, doesn't like women—particularly Black women. Now, he would never flat out say he hates Black women, but his actions and commentary over the years prove otherwise.

"My dad's complaints about his mother, sisters, and other women in his life are all that they are loud, bossy, mean, and angry. That's probably why he married my mother, who is very mild mannered and practically a doormat at times. Couple that with his belief that the Bible commands women to be silent and submit in all things to their husbands, and you have a home where girls are taught both directly and indirectly never to speak up, lest they be seen as ungodly Sapphires."

As a result, Liz has always been quiet and reserved, often to her own detriment.

"It's funny that I'm probably one of the most introverted and meek women most people have ever met, yet my silence is confused with anger. On the rare occasions when I do speak up for myself, I'm accused of being an angry Black woman."

Liz notes a conversation with a supervisor when she was repeatedly urged, "Don't get upset."

"I didn't raise my voice or have an angry tone the entire time I spoke to [her]. Of course, like a normal human being, hearing 'don't get upset' actually makes me upset because I'm not being heard."

Black women *do* get angry. Everyone does. But the angry Black woman stereotype denies them their warranted rage.

"You know how y'all are."

A friendly plumber tossed this gem from under my bathroom sink while sharing a tale about calming his wife—a Black woman—who was angry at a client for attempting to stiff their small business. I hoped that "how [Black women] are" referred to the type of people who become reasonably upset when someone undervalues their hard work and threatens their family's livelihood, as any business owner would. It didn't.

Black Witch says the characterization of Black women as irrationally angry is frustrating because "A lot of things that Black women talk about are valid issues. But the angry White guy gets a show on CBS, NBC, Fox News. He gets to be the head of the Congress. If he's an angry White guy, he's passionate. If he's an angry Black man, he's militant, but he's a leader.

"It's really degrading, because it doesn't allow you to feel. There's nothing you're supposed to be angry about. A lot of our anger comes from not being listened to. [People] ignore our problems and think we're crazy—just foaming at the mouth."

Writer Deesha Philyaw grew up around women who had many legitimate reasons to be angry. And she admits to once associating a certain sort of anger with Black womanhood—even trading on it herself as a young girl.

"In my teen years, I had a no-nonsense persona that masked a lot of insecurities and self-doubt. I was all talk and bluster. Looking back on it, I suspect that I was mimicking some of the Black women I knew—friends of my family who would physically fight people when they were angry. They cussed someone out at least once a week. Often, their partners and ex-partners bore the brunt of their behavior. Sometimes it was White folks at work.

"At the opposite end of the spectrum were the women in my family. They were long suffering, often doormats for the sons, brothers, and lovers in their lives. I loved these women, but their unhappiness was palpable, and I didn't want that for myself. I was also too chicken shit and too much of a softie to be cussing people out and fighting," she laughs.

But Deesha stresses that the women she knew who were easily angered and aggressive were not "angry Black women" to her. In other words, they were not defined by their need for better coping mechanisms.

"I thought of them as Black women. And I was committed to being a different kind of Black woman: I wouldn't act out and be controlled by my anger, but I wasn't going to be anyone's doormat either. I've never worried about anyone applying the label to me, nor have I kept quiet for fear of being labeled. Only recently, through social media, have I learned that this trope is being used to stifle Black women's justifiable expressions of anger and to paint a picture of Black woman aggression where there is none.

"As an adult, I disagree that this is a Black thing, or a woman thing. I assume that anyone, regardless of race, who has those frustrations and limitations, and few coping skills and resources, would and does act the same way. It's just that Black women seem to have had it codified: neck-rolling, side-eyeing, finger-pointing, and our own glossary of 'reading' terms."

Liz says, "Yes, I'm angry. I'm angry because I can't and don't know how to express my anger. I'm angry because all of my feelings and my sisters' feelings—hurt, pain, joy, accomplishment—are met with derision.

"I'm angry that someone like Shonda Rhimes can be maligned in the most respected newspaper in the country because there were no Black female editors at the *New York Times* who could've said 'This is ridiculous. Try again.'

"I'm angry that Black men don't seem to have our backs. I'm angry that Dean Baquet [executive editor at the *New York Times*] basically Kanye-shrugged and defended [Alessandra Stanley]. I'm angry that [Stanley] herself blamed Black women for being too stupid to get her point. I'm angry that when Shonda Rhimes justifiably claps back, many people think she's living up to the angry Black woman stereotype."

Our anger and aggression are even unwanted in environments where those emotions are expected, according to Kimberly "Bunny" Hopson, a former reporter who is retired from the Roller Derby scene.[13]

"If you're Black and an aggressive player, which I am, you're automatically branded as dangerous, scary, and mean."

I should remind the reader here that Roller Derby is a *contact* sport.

"Yeah, okay, just because I knock you on your ass and have a serious look in my eye when I run you down, doesn't mean I'm going to knife you, break your skate plates, and steal your purse.

"Once you've received that brand, even for one exhibition bout, all of the referees in the tristate area know you and are wary. I have a reputation, apparently," laments the five-foot-nothing Bunny.

"It's pointless, but I really do try to tone myself down during games. The thing is that Roller Derby is practically born for the promotion of an alter ego. Who I am on the track is a facet of my personality, but not the central part. I can't even help being aggressive.

"I am extremely focused on one task: knocking you down, whoever you are. Many teams call on me to sub or play for them because of it, but it's as much a curse as it is a blessing. In any given game, I'm fouled out or ejected before the second half because of nit-picking from refs who just know for sure that I pushed some girl down in cold blood. I'm still a high-penalty player even when I'm not ejected.

"White players can curse, cheat, kick, and do whatever else they want, so long as they stay White. But me? I get called on stuff I don't even do sometimes."

Perceptions of our anger leave us vulnerable in more important places than the roller rink.

- -

Moments in Alright

Black women hold about two-thirds of all bachelor's and doctorate degrees awarded to African Americans.[14]

- -

Swallowing Anger, Losing Respect

Tracy Elba,* thirty-nine, was a producer with a postgraduate degree and a shelf full of awards when she got called up to the TV news big leagues—a job in a top-three market. Even with more than a decade of experience under her belt, she was unprepared for what she encountered. Newsrooms are notoriously high pressure and fast paced, but this . . .

"It was seriously dysfunctional," Tracy says. "People screamed, slammed things, got in each other's faces and cussed at each other. I say *cussed* not cursed. It was hostile. Granted, it's easy to feel slammed in that kind of environment. But out of the four newsrooms where I've worked, this was the worst place. You had to be tough to survive and willing to take a whole lot of shit."[15]

She entered her new gig a superstar. The ratings on her show were great. By chance, she caught breaking news on her cell phone one afternoon and saw her footage lead the evening news. The station's president and general manager seemed to love her and stopped by her desk each day to say hello. But, she says, too much public praise made her a target in the competitive environment. She found herself on the wrong side of a powerful executive producer.

"He buried me with assignments, then enumerated mistakes in my unfinished work and sent them to higher ups. He yelled at me and demeaned me—treated me horribly. I was the only Black person on his team, and I felt like I had no allies.

"I didn't go to HR. That's the thing that I didn't do. I wanted to be strong. I thought I could power through it. I thought I could solve the problem by using my smartness, my niceness, and my contacts. I thought I could get ahead of it."

And she didn't want to be an angry Black woman. Tracy admits that many of her colleagues went toe-to-toe with senior producers—bumping heads in the newsroom and sharing drinks later. But she didn't feel that path was open to her. And it seems she was right.

"One day, after a show, he cursed me out in front of everyone— a whole row of producers. It got so bad that another producer was begging him to stop. I had had it. I raised my voice: 'You will NOT talk to me like this. I know you're my boss. But you'll never, ever talk to me like this in front of everyone ever again.'

"He slammed his hand on the desk and walked away. I got in trouble for yelling at him—disrespecting my supervisor. From there on out, every time anyone would yell at me, I would just take it. People had said, 'When he does that, you just have to give it back to him.' A Black woman can't do that and expect for the results to still be positive."

Tracy insists she's not a crier, "but that newsroom would send me home crying every day." Her hair began falling out and her milk dried up, keeping her from nursing her six-month-old baby.

"Those people hated me—they hated my *soul*. I had never had that. I was used to shining. This is the first time that I felt like a failure. After work one day, I went over to my sister's house. I told her 'I just don't know who to be in that newsroom. If I curse somebody out, I'm in trouble. If I take it, I'm in trouble.'"

Tracy, who used to rock a full-size Afro, laughs ruefully: "My sister thought maybe if I straightened my hair, they would like me better."

Not long after the incident with her executive producer, Tracy was fired.

"The day they let me go, I cried in the parking lot. I didn't let them see me. But it was a relief. Being fired was better than quitting. I would never have quit. I knew how hard I tried. I knew I had given my all.

"I never thought I would see myself in an unemployment line. I had more experience, more education, and more accolades than anyone in that newsroom."

One month later, she had a new job.

"I'm killing it there," she smiles. "I have my confidence back."

But the experience taught her something.

"Those people were crazy and dysfunctional," she says. "I'm not an angry Black woman. I don't have to curse anybody out. But I do have a right to stand up for myself. I do have a right to be treated with respect—to demand respect. I wasn't wrong for doing that. We are never wrong for doing that."

Chapter 6

Strength
Precious Mettle

In the Summer 2014 issue of *Bitch* magazine, I wrote about a stereotype that both buoys and burdens Black women.[1] With shades of Sapphire's hardness, the myth embodies the idea of African American women as perpetually tough and uniquely indestructible.

Strong. Black. Woman.

The words fit together like Blue Magic, sizzling hot combs, and Sunday afternoon.

We are the fighters and the women who don't take shit from no man. We are the sassy women with the sharp tongues and hands firmly on our hips. We are the ride-or-die chicks. We are the women who have, like Sojourner Truth, "plowed and planted and gathered into barns and no man could head me." We are the mothers who make a way out of no way. On TV, we are the no-nonsense police chiefs and judges. We are the First Ladies with the impressive biceps.

But there is a dirty side to the perceived uncommon strength of Black women. Ultimately, the "strong Black woman" stereotype is an albatross, at odds with African American women's very survival. Because, according to pop culture and media, we are also the workhorses. We are the cold, overeducated, career-obsessed sisters who will never marry. We are the indefatigable mamas who don't need help, the castrating harpies. We are the brawling Worldstar "hood rats." We are the women and girls who are unrapeable, whom no one need worry about when we go missing. We are the scary bogeywomen on America's doorstep in the middle of the night. And, too often, we are the women who dare not give in to our vulnerability, even as we're breaking, emotionally and physically.

Stories of Black families are filled with sacrificing ma'dears and mamas, whose ability to nurture and work was seemingly limitless. Too often Black families lose sight of these women as human beings, and in efforts to emulate them, Black women dash their own health and well-being on the rocks. They come to believe, to their detriment, that preternatural strength means that Black women can and should bear any physical and emotional burden without complaint.

Of course, Black women's strength is also blamed for the Black marriage crisis. Singer Robin Thicke shared more unasked-for advice in a late 2011 *Essence* article, when he told Black women to take better care of their men: "Maybe you're being too stubborn. Maybe you're not saying you're sorry. You have to take good care of him, too. You have to give love to get love."[2] Maybe we're being too damned strong for our own good. The consensus seems to be that Black women are too tough to love or be loved.

Still, many women find undeniable truth, liberation, and empowerment in the "strong Black woman" meme. Heidi Renée

Lewis says, "There are times when I assume that Black woman resilience—the kind that allows you to face racism and sexism and heterosexism on a daily basis and still maintain your sanity and your health. I love that part of the strength that Black women have had to have. That strength is real."

· ·

Moments in Alright

Black women have a strong work ethic. Among all women, they have the highest rate of workforce participation.[3]

· ·

Black (Woman) Power

Sixty-year-old Deborah Latham-White remembers embracing the idea of Black female strength as a teen at the dawn of the Black Power movement.[4] "Black women were disrupting American beauty culture. We were starting to wear our hair natural as a political statement of acceptance and self-love." But the currency of cultural strength wasn't just halos of kinky hair and Afro-chic sartorial tastes. "We were also throwing up our fists in a sign of solidarity with the Black Power movement, as well as being actively engaged in struggle," she says. Who would not want to be Angela Davis, Fannie Lou Hamer, Ruby Dee, Audre Lorde, Shirley Chisholm?

Today, loving profiles of former First Lady Michelle Obama often focus on her personal and professional strength, particularly her exceptional education and career achievements, her egalitarian marriage, and her athleticism. An online search for "Michelle

Obama" and "strong" reveals a host of images with America's former First Lady flexing her impressively toned biceps. The former FLOTUS is positioned as a "strong Black woman," both literally and figuratively, making her a modern role model and icon not just to other Black women and girls but to other Americans as well.

Black women look to strong female figures for motivation. They evoke the historical strength of their foremothers to tell each other "You can do it." Adrianne Traylor says she is moved by the strength of her late grandmother, a devoutly religious rural Texan who farmed alongside her husband while working other jobs and raising nine children.[5] She left school after the eighth grade, but seven of her children would go on to receive college degrees. "Her example transferred a desire for aspiration and achievement to succeeding generations. She is the embodiment of the best of what 'strong Black woman' can mean."

Blogger Erika Nicole Kendall has found many Black women unwilling to let go of the idea of strength as part of their identity. When she challenges the myth, it is nearly always met with debate.

"[Some women say,] 'I actually take pride in being strong, why would you want to take that from me?'"

The key, Kendall says, is realizing "I am strong and I am powerful, but I am also vulnerable and I am also able to break and because of that I should be very careful with myself and expect the people around me to be careful with me as well—to support me, help me, provide encouragement, and provide some kind of relief."

And that is the problem—at least part of it. It is easy to forget that people who are strong need support and relief. It is sometimes depressingly hard for even Black women to remember that they are not, indeed, superwomen.

"I've had to be a strong Black woman since I was seven," Fatima Thomas[*] says, "Even when I didn't want to be, I've always had to be.[6]

"I had a mom who was an alcoholic. She was on drugs. She was left by her husband and she checked out of life. She partied and had fun. I had to take care of my siblings—I mean feeding, getting [them] dressed for school, the whole situation. I've always been that."

For Fatima, surviving her childhood required remarkable strength. But one can survive and still be in pain, broken. A survivor can still need help.

One night, Fatima found herself perched in the middle of a highway wearing all black—a strong girl at the end of her rope. "I tried to commit suicide. I remember sitting in the middle of the highway just kind of daring something to hit me so that I wouldn't have to live anymore. I'm so young that I don't realize that if you're sitting in the middle of the highway, neither side is going to hit you. I sat in the middle of the highway, so traffic is veering around me. I'm like, 'Okay, I guess I'll go home and deal with that again.'"

She tried again in college. "I took every pill between my room and my cheating boyfriend's dorm room. Every pill I could find, I took it and I lived through it—barely, but I did. I lived through it. Years later, I had a botched abortion and I lived through that. I was on life support. It seemed like no matter what, God wasn't going to let me die, so I had to endure stuff.

"Within the last three or four years, I have had walking pneumonia three times. I've had kidney stones. I'm convinced I have had depression, even though I haven't been diagnosed. I thoroughly attribute all that to strong Black womanhood.

"I'm convinced that because [Black women] persevere and make it through, nobody's paying attention to what we're going through when it's happening. I don't think the idea of the strong Black woman is just a burden, I think it is killing us.

"Once you become a mother, you will survive for that kid. If you love that kid, and especially if you love that kid more than you love yourself, it doesn't matter what it takes. There have been days where, except for getting my children fed and dressed and out the door, I was not out of the bed. My children didn't even realize it, because while they were gone, I was in the bed, depressed, on and off sleep, couldn't get up. Here comes the bus. I drag myself out of the bed, go cook dinner, get back in the bed.

"There are moments when everything around here's going good. I'm getting awards. I'm getting praise. And I feel like, 'When are they going to realize I'm a complete phony?' I just want to go back to bed. I don't want to do this because what if I'm not strong? What if I want to cry? What if I want to admit that things hurt? Who do I admit that to? When you've been so strong so long, even when you do break down and someone is there, you're on the floor saying, 'Somebody help me' and they'll be like, 'Oh, girl, get up. You got this.' No I don't. That's why I'm on the floor . . . I don't got this."

• •

Moments in Alright

Tired of taking her children to Philadelphia or Manhattan for cultural activities, Taneshia Nash Laird founded the Baker Street Social Club to support and promote artists, writers, and performers and bring the arts and cultures of the African diaspora to her hometown of Princeton, New Jersey.[7]

• •

Built Black Girl Tough

Lisa Patton, fifty, says, "When people perceive you as the strong Black woman, they don't think of you as being a complete human being. They think that you don't have vulnerabilities, that you don't hurt, you just kind of soldier on. Everyone expects that out of you. It is what society expects out of you. It is what your family has basically raised you to be, because in many African American families, the girls are raised to basically do what they need to do."[8]

Deborah Latham-White agrees that Black women often pass down the idea of strength at all costs to younger generations out of a love that is perhaps misguided.

"Lots of times, our own mothers get that geared up in their heads: 'I've got to make my daughter tough, because it's a tough world out there.'"

For centuries, the notion of Black female strength has also been used to challenge our humanity and femininity. Long after the era of the cult of true womanhood, by the age of the Equal Rights Amendment, when middle-class White women fought to come down off the pedestal of idealized womanhood and progressive folks celebrated the strength of various marginalized peoples, Black women were still seen as *uniquely* tough.

"Black Woman Power," an interesting but flawed article by second-wave feminist Caroline Bird in the March 10, 1969, issue of *New York* magazine, deems Black women capable and independent (read: strong) by necessity.[9] Black women fight, Bird says, because they have no one to fight for them, unlike women with proximity to White, patriarchal power. "Whatever the reasons, the fact is that Negro women in America have escaped some of the psyche-crippling education of white girls. They haven't been carefully taught how *not* to fight. On the contrary, some of them fight hard and develop a personal style of fighting that suggests that 'grace under pressure' which is supposed to be the essence of courage."

Bird's piece spins allegedly distinctive Black female strength as a powerful weapon, giving African American women an edge over White women and Black men—a dubious message. It also paints Black women as possessing a durability that is nearly inhuman. For instance, Bird asserts that the "absence of Negro fathers hurts growing boys more than girls, and saved Negro girls from some of the dissatisfactions with their sex that have brought many white women to psychoanalysis." Abandoning Black girls does not hurt them, this view suggests; instead, it improbably makes them stronger. Bird also pits Black female achievement against Black male success ("Without half trying, Negro women are better able than their men to cope"), unintentionally illustrating the double bind that strong Black women face: in a society where strength and power are reserved for White people and men most of all, Black women are always at the precipice of overstepping their bounds.

Society remains uneasy with female strength of any stripe and still prefers and champions delicate damsels—an outdated sentiment that limits all women. But because the damsel's face is still viewed as unequivocally White and female, it is a particular problem for Black women. As long as vulnerability and softness are the basis for acceptable femininity (and acceptable femininity is a requirement for a woman's life to have value), women who are perpetually framed because of their race as supernaturally indestructible will not be viewed with regard.

This may be why we so rarely see the Black women who are victims of violence on true-crime television, despite the fact that Black women are more likely to be victims of sexual violence and domestic homicidal violence. Instead, we overwhelmingly see young White women who fit the picture of idealized true womanhood (journalist Gwen Ifill coined the phrase "missing white woman syndrome" to describe this disparate media attention).[10] Young, blond Natalee Holloway and mommy-to-be Laci Peterson are damsels, beneficiaries of sympathetic national media attention and a drive for justice; Tamika Huston and Latoyia Figueroa, Black women who disappeared under identical circumstances, are not.

Sheri Parks, an associate professor at the University of Maryland, described the significance of this reporting bias in a 2006 appearance on CNN, explaining that stories about missing women capture the national attention, "uniting people to save a soul." The woman "becomes a symbol, and if we save her for a few days, we're okay."[11] If lack of media coverage is any indication, the media does not believe strong Black women need saving.

But lack of empathy for Black women has other serious implications. When Staten Island mother Glenda Moore's car became submerged by water during Hurricane Sandy in 2012, she was able to free her children, little boys ages two and four, from their car seats only to have the rushing water sweep them away. When the distraught Moore attempted to garner help from her neighbors—to simply convince them to call 911—she found only closed doors. Said one neighbor, before shutting the door in Moore's face, "I don't know you."[12]

In response to news coverage of the tragedy, a commenter at the *Christian Post* defended Moore's neighbors, asking "How many people are going to let a muscular, screaming Black woman into their house? How would you know whether it was just a trick and you were about to be the victim of home invasion, robbery, rape. . . . That is the problem, you just don't know."[13]

Lest this comment sound like just your average internet troll, consider what happened when nineteen-year-old Renisha McBride knocked on Theodore Wafer's door in the early morning of November 2, 2013. McBride was seeking help at Wafer's suburban Detroit home after a car accident, but instead of receiving aid she was shot in the face.[14]

On her blog, writer DJ Freedom Fighter responded to the transformation of five-foot-three-inch, 130-pound Moore from distraught mother to burly, duplicitous beast, calling it "optic Whiteness."[15] The blogger could also have been discussing Renisha McBride. Optic Whiteness allowed Moore's neighbor (and Wafer) to "permissibly deny her help that he would have certainly offered to someone who embodies a picturesque version of the standards of womanhood and motherhood."

Following the Moore and McBride tragedies, a 2013 article in *Time* asked "Why are Black women seen as more threatening, more masculine and less in need of help?"[16] UCLA historian Sarah Haley answered, "Black women have been seen as different than Black men, certainly, but they have not always been seen as women either; to be a woman is to be seen as deserving of protection, and Black women are not always seen that way."

If public attention is any indicator, though, Black women are seen as unworthy faces of violence against women *and* Black people. Couple stereotypes about Black women's hardness with the historic devaluing of women and it explains why even amid a national war against violence on Black bodies, Black femmes are often forgotten.

Say Her Name

In the early hours of March 13, 2020, officers executed a search warrant on the home of twenty-six-year-old Breonna Taylor, a young Black medical worker in Louisville. Authorities believed that an ex-boyfriend, who was under police investigation, may have used the house to receive drugs. Taylor and her current boyfriend Kenneth Walker were roused from their bed by a battering ram pounding their door. The couple feared intruders. As the door gave way, Walker shot once from a licensed gun, wounding one officer. Police fired several rounds, hitting Taylor five times. She did not receive medical attention for twenty minutes.

In a recorded call to 911, Walker says, "I don't know what's happening. Someone kicked in the door and shot my girlfriend."

Breonna Taylor was killed. No drugs were found at her home.[17]

Like Black men and boys, Black women and girls are victims of a racist police state.

Black women are disproportionately targeted by law enforcement. According to the African American Policy Forum (AAPF), "in New York City—one of the jurisdictions with the most extensive data collection on police stops—the rates of racial disparities in stops, frisks, and arrests are identical for Black men and Black women."[18]

Police violence is commonly defined in ways that obscure harm to Black women, including sexual and gender-based abuse, like that committed by Daniel Holtzclaw, a former Oklahoma City Police Department officer convicted in 2015 on multiple counts of rape, sexual battery, forcible oral sodomy, and other sexual charges.[19] All of Holtzclaw's suspected victims were Black women, chosen for the vulnerability caused by their race, class, and former involvement with law enforcement.[20] According to a report on anti-transgender violence, more than a third of Black trans women who interact with law enforcement are assumed by police to be sex workers, leading to harassment, abuse, and mistreatment.[21]

Black women are disproportionately killed by law enforcement, though they are routinely ignored in data about police killings. Black women slain by law enforcement are not likely to receive justice. The *New York Times* reports that nearly fifty Black women have been killed by police since 2015.[22] There have been charges in only two cases. One officer was acquitted. One case remained pending as of September 2020. No one was charged for killing Breonna Taylor, though a grand jury did indict a detective involved in her shooting for endangering Taylor's neighbors whose apartment was hit by bullets that missed their target.[23]

Mike Brown. Trayvon Martin. Eric Garner. Their unconscionable deaths provoked national outcry—a movement. Atatiana Jefferson. Pamela Turner. Yvette Smith. Aiyana Stanley-Jones.[24] Their names and stories dissolved from public consciousness like paper in the rain. It seemed, at first, that this would also be Breonna Taylor's fate. It took the killing of George Floyd, almost two months later, to galvanize national attention and ignite a summer of protest, including demands for #JusticeforBreonna.

According to the AAPF, "Black women who are profiled, beaten, sexually assaulted, and killed by law enforcement officials are conspicuously absent from this frame even when their experiences are identical. When their experiences with police violence are distinct—uniquely informed by race, gender, gender identity, and sexual orientation—Black women remain invisible."[25]

In 2014, the organization launched #SayHerName, a campaign designed to "shed light on Black women's experiences of police violence in an effort to support a gender-inclusive approach to racial justice that centers all Black lives equally."[26]

Black women are erased from discourse and demonstrations around state violence, even as they are leading the fight for justice from law enforcement. It was three Black women—Alicia

Garza, Patrisse Cullors, and Opal Tometi—who founded Black Lives Matter in 2013, following the acquittal of George Zimmerman in the killing of Trayvon Martin.[27] And in the summer of 2020, when millions of people worldwide took to the streets to protest the killings of George Floyd and Breonna Taylor, Black women were often at the forefront of the revolution—lending their strength to the movement, while remaining vulnerable and unprotected themselves.

Nineteen-year-old Oluwatoyin Salau protested in her hometown of Tallahassee, Florida. She organized in the memory of George Floyd and Tony McDade—a Black transgender man who was killed by a Tallahassee police officer. There is a photo of Toyin, as she was known, flanked by fellow Black Lives Matter activists in front of the Tallahassee Police Department.[28] Her face is contorted with passion. Behind her, signs read "No Justice. No Peace." A month after the photo was taken, Salau tweeted about being sexually assaulted by a man who had offered her a ride. Then she went missing.[29]

In the wake of her disappearance, a video of Salau, giving one of her impassioned speeches, was shared widely on Twitter. "Right now, our lives matter, Black lives matter . . . We are doing this for our brothers and our sisters who got shot, but we are doing this for every Black person."

Oluwatoyin Salau's body would be found along with the body of another woman—seventy-five-year-old Victoria Sims—in a home on Tallahassee's southeast side. The women had been murdered.

In news coverage following her death, those who knew Salau remembered how she would often recite the names of Black victims of police violence.

"I don't want their names gone in vain," she said.

Say her name—Oluwatoyin Salau.

Moments in Alright

Black women do camp, climb, and hike—just ask Rue Mapp, whose love of nature was sparked growing up in Northern California. Rue was dismayed to see few other Black people on her forays into the great outdoors, so she founded Outdoor Afro, a social organization that connects African Americans nationwide with outdoor activities such as birding, fishing, gardening, and skiing.[30]

Finding the Balance

Heidi Renée Lewis says, "I am raising a daughter. The reality is, a certain kind of strength will be required for her to make it through this life with her sanity and health—to not let racism and sexism kill her. But I have to be very careful about telling her to be strong, because I also want her to be fully human."

Sofia Quintero, creator of the Feminist Love Project, a tele-summit on feminism and love, concurs, saying that there are times when she embraces the idea of strong Black womanhood "as a way to practice resiliency and protect myself. But the flip side is that it allows little space for me to be vulnerable, seek support, and otherwise be fully human."[31]

And that is what the enduring meme of the "strong Black woman" obscures: it makes it harder for others to see Black women as complex beings. Worse, the myth of Black women's extraordinary strength makes it difficult for Black women to see themselves.

The most radical thing African American women can do is to throw off the shackles forged by the strong Black woman meme and regain a full and complex humanity that allows them to be capable, strong, and independent but also to be carried and cared for. Allowing for physical and emotional vulnerability is not weakness; it is humanness. More, it is the revolutionary act in the face of a society eager to mold Black women into hard, unbreakable things.

"Understanding that being strong and being the only one to manage everything—we do that out of necessity and maybe we do want to be proud of that," Erika Nicole Kendall says. "But we have to monitor what we allow that to mean in terms of how we care for ourselves. It's not, 'Oh, I can handle anything so I'm going to handle everything.' It's, 'I can do this, but I also need to be realistic about how it's going to affect me in the end and I need to plan and prepare for that.'"

Chapter 7

Health
Fat, Sick, and Crazy

The Centers for Disease Control and Prevention reports that 57 percent of African American women over the age of twenty are obese.[1] One in four Black women over fifty-five has diabetes.[2] Heart disease is more prevalent among Black women than White women.[3] Thirty-seven percent of Black women have high blood pressure.[4] Women are more likely than men to experience major depression, but Black women are half as likely as their White counterparts to seek treatment.[5] Persistent stereotypes help explain why the public processes these health challenges with more parts blame and exasperation than compassion, believing that Black women are simply fat, sick, and crazy rather than human beings in need of help.

It's the Racism, Stupid

Too little attention is paid to the ways systemic inequity diminishes the physical and mental well-being of Black people, even though research suggests that living Black in America is a unique health stressor.

Black women face racism and sexism and often carry disproportionate responsibilities, which can place their bodies in a constant state of hypervigilance, anxiety, and worry. This results in real physiological damage, called "allostatic load," the overburdening of bodily systems, including those regulating blood sugar, circulation, mood, and other processes.[6]

Researchers believe this helps explain several negative health outcomes for Black Americans, including high maternal and infant mortality rates and high rates of chronic illnesses like the ones previously mentioned.[7] It also made Black Americans, including Black women, more vulnerable during the COVID-19 pandemic.[8]

According to the Centers for Disease Control, Black Americans were 1.1 times more likely than White Americans to contract the virus, 2.9 times more likely to be hospitalized, and 1.9 times more likely to die.[9] And, because of other disparities, Black people were more likely be mentally burdened by the pandemic. A study into the effects of COVID on pregnant women, published by the National Institutes of Health, found that "Black pregnant women reported greater likelihood of having their employment negatively impacted, more concerns about a lasting economic burden, and more worries about their prenatal care, birth experience, and post-natal needs."[10]

And a study published by the National Institutes of Health in 2012 revealed that "Black-white disparities in mortality persist after adjustment for socioeconomic status and health behaviors."[11] Even in the best of circumstances—when a Black woman has the access and ability to give her body the best care—her health outcomes are likely to be worse than those of her White sisters.

Racism is a public health issue that is too often overlooked in favor of chastising Black women doing the best they can.

Wake Up!

Sometimes bodies don't need fixing so much as care. Even if they are sick. Even if they are disabled. Too often, the expectation that Black women live up to the strong Black woman myth means they are denied that care, but also fail to show compassion to themselves.

One day, when she was forty years old, Deborah Latham-White had an anxiety attack and felt as if she were dying.[12]

"My heart was pounding so hard, I assumed I was having a heart attack."

That day she found herself sitting in the office of a mental health practitioner who suggested that she also get a complete physical. It revealed dangerously low iron levels. In fact, she was so anemic that she fainted outside the clinic. And doctors discovered something else, too—uterine fibroid tumors.

Deborah had been ignoring signs that her mental and physical health was fragile, thinking she could work through the many symptoms that had been plaguing her.

"The women on my mom's side of the family always have hysterectomies by the time they're in their early forties," Deborah says. "I should have been listening to what my body was saying."

Following weeks of improving health, she was finally able to have a partial hysterectomy. It took four more months to heal, giving Deborah time to question how she became so sick. The answer, in part, was that she had become, as Zora Neale Hurston wrote of Black women in *Their Eyes Were Watching God*, "de mule uh de world," taking on everyone's burdens to her detriment.

A change was in order.

While recovering, Deborah spent time doing more of the things she loves to do, including reading and watching movies. She started treating herself to what she calls "Queen Esther Days," all about pampering. She started taking naps. And she learned how to say no.

"I changed how I responded to some people in my life. 'You're in a crisis, I'm so sad for you. I can't help you. If I can I'll let you know.' I used to feel guilty when I would say, 'No, I *can't*.' Now I can say, 'No, I don't *want* to.'"

Deborah says that it took "skidding like this healthwise" for her to realize that she is not invincible. And that was a hard lesson to learn within a culture that wants most for Black women to be self-sacrificing Mammies.

"We are taught to take care of everybody else. We are always giving our strength away. You know what I'm saying? We're strong for our children. We're strong on the job. We're strong if we're in church. It's always an outpouring.

"We're never allowed to say, 'Hey, I'm really tired. Hey, I'm hurting. I'm exhausted. You're exhausting me. I need a break. I don't want to do anything for anybody.' We're just geared to give."

. . . .

Moments in Alright

Tricia Hersey believes that rest is a form of resistance and that sleep deprivation is a racial and social justice issue. She founded The Nap Ministry in 2016 to "help deprogram the masses from grind culture." The Ministry uses social media, art, and community organizing to uplift the liberating and healing power of naps.[13]

• •

More than twenty years later, Deborah is happy to have survived her wake-up call, but for several of her friends, it came too late.

"In my personal sister-friend group, I've lost three friends. They died really fast. They were all 'strong Black women' who ended up not reading their own health signals. One of them had different health problems all through her life. She just finally wore herself out.

"I had a supervisor who had two thousand hours of sick time, who was doubled over in chronic pain. She said, 'I can't take off from work.' When she finally does go [to the doctor], because it gets to the point where the pain can't be managed anymore, she finds out that she has terminal cancer. She's actually dying."

Deborah says many Black women believe that if we aren't there—at home, at church, in our community groups, at work—everything will fall apart. "I don't believe that anymore. It's not healthy."

Privileging her health and well-being takes on particular resonance as Deborah ages. She is in her mid-sixties now and sees the toll that lifetimes of personal neglect can take on Black women. The Sapphire-influenced idea of the always-feisty older Black woman is a myth.

"I've really started to tune out what society says aging should be for me. Instead, I've been looking at people like my mother and her social circle and how they're handling being old—their health issues, their finances, and things like that.

"Before, where I might have just gone to the doctor and been quiet and listened and said, 'Okay,' now it's more like, 'Wait, I need to ask you these questions. Do you mind if I write down what you're saying or record it, because it's a lot to be taken in?'

"I took an online course on aging. It just gave me an entirely different perspective on the subject itself. But it didn't address Black people. That's critical now, because a lot of Black women are not realizing the later years of our lives can be lived really differently.

"I'm not interested in being forty [again]. I was very different mentally at forty *and* physically. At forty, I was really strong; it almost killed me. I admit that. I had too much on my plate. [Even now,] I'm constantly in the door and out the door. I'm here. I'm there. I'm sure that that's part of fitting that strong Black woman image. I don't think you ever just totally break away from it. What you can do is manage it because it's not only ingrained in your mind but it's ingrained in the minds of other people."

Carrying the Weight

At the center of discussions about Black women's health is their high rate of obesity (based on BMI, which was never meant to be used as a marker for health and is not calibrated for Black folks or women[14]). According to Sabrina Strings in *Fearing the Black Body: The Racial Origins of Fat Phobia*, "The fear of the imagined 'fat Black woman' was created by racial and religious ideologies that have been used to both degrade Black women and discipline white women." Strings adds that fatness has been aligned with savagery—with "coarseness" and "immorality."[15]

Concern about fat Black women is less about their health and more that their fatness is viewed as a visual illustration of negative stereotypes. That is why when talk turns to African American women and fatness, the conversation tends to be punitive and tinged with ridicule instead of support for women who want to make lifestyle changes and "mind your fucking business" for the ones that don't.

In 2011, actor Boris Kodjoe caused a Twitter storm joking about "300-pound women in thongs, gnawing on chicken wings while grinding on me" and lecturing his largely Black female fan base on health.[16]

"No more excuses! High blood pressure and diabetes do not 'run in your family.' Pork chops, mac 'n' cheese, and tons of soda do! #stopitnow."

He also shared a list of what he termed "fat excuses," which included spending time watching the reality show *Keeping Up with the Kardashians* instead of working out.

Kodjoe may have meant well, but evoking the image of a chicken-eating Mammy Jezebel and blaming Black women's rate of obesity solely on laziness and lack of willpower misses the mark. Erika Nicole Kendall, founder of the website A Black Girl's Guide to Weight Loss, says these sorts of assessments "burn my toast. Oh, [they] burn my toast!"[17]

A compassionate eye toward Black women and an exploration of the systemic issues that underscore their physical challenges might open the door to improved health and reveal "we are not as complicit as people think we are."

Whole, unprocessed food may be healthier, but processed food can last longer and is often cheaper and faster to prepare.

Those qualities are important for all working women trying to make ends meet and feed their families, but they are especially important to Black women, who are more likely to work, to be single parents, and to live in poverty. In addition, some research shows that food deserts—urban neighborhoods and rural towns without ready access to fresh, healthy, and affordable food—disproportionately affect Black Americans.[18]

"How hard is it to get to where the healthy food is?" Erika asks. "When you go to your grocery store and you look in the produce aisle, are they properly keeping the produce? When you walk over there and you reach for an orange, do you see mold? Is the grocery store pleasant? Dirty? Do you see bugs there? Is your grocery store actually a glorified bodega? And when you get your food, how hard is it for you to get your groceries home?

"All of these are issues that heavily affect those of us with the least amount of money, and thanks to a history of racist policies in America, those of us with the least amount of money are Black."

Moments in Alright

Avid runners Toni Carey and Ashley Hicks founded Black Girls RUN! in 2009 when they found little support for their own running practice. By 2012, thousands of Black women were running with them through nearly seventy local groups across the country. The Black Girls RUN! platform supports women in getting active to combat obesity and chronic illness and to encourage mental and physical well-being.[19]

A 2012 study that revealed that two of every five African American women say they avoid exercise because of concerns about their hair caused no end of fat-Black-woman shaming.[20] But the issue is not pure vanity, Erika says, pointing to America's history of demonizing Black women's natural hair. Keeping textured Black hair straight means keeping it away from moisture that could make it revert to its natural kinky state. Restraightening hair can take considerable time, and repeated use of blow dryers and hot combs is damaging. At the same time, Black women are chastised for spending money on weaves and wigs. What is a woman who has been told that her hair as it grows from her head is unsightly and unprofessional to do if not avoid activities that might affect her hair in a way that gets her penalized?

Of course, the entire *nation*—not just Black women—is struggling with rising weight and failing health amid a culture of sedentary jobs, increased workloads, long commutes, drive-thrus, processed food, and poor health care. According to the Centers for Disease Control, more than one-third of adults in the United States are obese, and related conditions—such as heart disease, strokes, and type-2 diabetes—are some of the leading causes of preventable death.[21]

Dr. Virginia Banks Bright says "there is little incentive" to truly educate the American populace, much less Black women, on healthy habits, because "far too many stakeholders are making money" from our continued sickness.[22]

"Pharmaceutical companies are making lots of money selling hypertensive drugs. And do you know how many people are on dialysis? They are running them 24/7 now. Dialysis companies are benefiting. Nephrologists are benefiting. Food companies are benefiting."

Meanwhile, information about nutrition and fitness isn't easy for the average person to get. Virginia says that there is not enough easily processed information for people to know what and how much they are eating. And, she adds, "We [doctors] do not receive a lot of nutritional training. We are not trained in how to eat."

Nor do most doctors have time to give their patients proper nutritional counseling, concurs physician Elizabeth Ucheoma-Cofield.

None of this means that it is impossible for Black women to take control of their weight and health. Virginia lost seventy-five pounds and became a runner at the age of sixty after a lifetime of struggles with weight. Her wake-up call came when her weight put the health of her knees in jeopardy. Elizabeth lost the twenty pounds she gained after taking on a challenging job as a medical director and undergoing brain surgery.

Moments in Alright

GirlTrek was born in 2010, founded by two LA friends, T. Morgan Dixon and Vanessa Garrison, who bonded over their love for 2Pac and smothered pork chops. Vanessa once calculated the average life expectancy of the women in her family. It was sixty-six. The pair decided to challenge their friends to walk with them to "heal our bodies, inspire our daughters and reclaim the streets of our neighborhoods." Today, GirlTrek is the largest public health nonprofit for African American women and girls in the United States, with nearly one hundred thousand neighborhood walkers.

Erika Nicole Kendall is among the Black women challenging the useless way others talk about Black female bodies and helping sisters get empowered, educated, and healthy besides. As with beauty, fitness is another area where Black women have created something new in the absence of others caring about what they need.

"We are going into our own communities. We are offering boot-camp classes. We are offering demos. We are offering conversation. We are hosting events where we talk about these things. A lot of the more popular YouTubers that do natural living and health and wellness are women of color."

But the idea that Black women are indifferent to health and wellness means that our efforts are often ignored. Erika tells of attending an event where the owner of a fitness studio effusively thanked her for attending.

"He's like, 'Yo, I'm really glad to see you out here 'cause you know, Black women—they don't work out like that.'"

That's probably news to the more than one hundred thousand women who visit the site A Black Girl's Guide to Weight Loss each month. Visitors include many non-Black women who enjoy the opportunity to congregate, learn, and offer each other support and encouragement. But the website holds a specific appeal for African American women happy to find a place online that speaks specifically to them in language that is frank and affirming.

"I talk about being poor and coming from a project in Cleveland and moving to the suburbs as a teen and then now living in New York as a professional writer," says Erika, adding that many Black women not only can relate to her personal story but also appreciate her vulnerability. "Even if you can't relate to the experiences, you can understand the humanity and that's not something that we often see or are allowed to see Black women display in public media."

Her readers know that Erika understands how challenging becoming healthy can be. She has lost a total of 176 pounds. More importantly, she changed how she treats her body: she learned to eat better and to move her muscles. Today, Erika has received certification as a personal trainer, with additional certifications in nutrition, weight loss, and women's fitness, from the National Academy of Sports Medicine. She says that she is "very slowly taking the steps to pursue a doctorate in epidemiology," to help better connect disparities in wellness to disparities in economics.

The results have been liberating, she says. She no longer has to grab the top of her car door to pull herself out of the driver's seat.

"I remember the day that I could get out without doing that, and every single day since then I jump up. Whenever I have to stand up from sitting, I will just jump up just because I'm like, 'I'm so glad I can do this now.'"

She can run. She's more agile. Her balance has improved. And she's strong.

"I have multiple bookshelves and I'm constantly rearranging my living room. I can do that by myself. My husband comes home and he's like, 'Did you have someone help you get the house like this?' And I'm like, 'Nope, did it myself.' I feel good. I feel capable. And I think that's the most important thing, that feeling of capability—the feeling that I can do it on my own. That's so powerful. That's a self-esteem booster right there."

Self-esteem is not the enemy of good health. Despite propaganda that tells Black women they are ugly, they still can manage to love themselves. That is a blessing rather than a curse. A 2012 study revealed that although Black women are heavier than White women, they have "appreciably higher self-esteem."

It found that 41 percent of average-size or thin White women reported having high self-esteem, while that figure was 66 percent among Black women considered by government standards to be overweight or obese.

The correct response to this finding, Erika says, is not "How dare these Black women think that they are attractive" but instead to probe how damaging strict beauty standards must be that even the women who represent the pinnacle of beauty in America can feel bad about themselves. But asking that question requires probing the negative effects of patriarchy in America. And we don't want to do that.

Many women in Black communities don't grow up having thinness associated with beauty, Erika says. "We didn't grow up feeling that we had to be bone thin in order to be attractive. We didn't grow up being told over and over that you won't get a husband if he can see a love handle. But my White girlfriends back home in Indiana? They absolutely received messaging like that. And they bent over backwards—and sometimes forward over a toilet—in order to make sure that they maintained that.

"I don't think we got that message and I don't think we need it. If we need anything, I think we need to understand that self-love is not just having a fresh hairdo, fresh nails, shoes, and a fly outfit. We need to understand that self-love should also incorporate taking care of our health. We can teach that without making it punitive, cruel, or insensitive."

Instead, in Erika's experience, what will help Black women collectively achieve good health is education, love, and support, and not just as these relate to *physical* fitness.

"We all need a mental escape every once and a while, and I think that having people around who understand, [who say] 'Listen, if I don't give her a break she's going to snap. If I don't help her out what is her future going to look like? What are her kids' futures going to look like?' A village is about more than [caring for] children. It's about good friends. It's about support. It's about having loved ones who actually display love and are not just burdens or frustrations."

Killer Secrets

In 2003, the California Black Women's Health Project found that only 7 percent of Black women with symptoms of mental illness seek treatment.[23] And, according to a 2009 National Institutes of Health manuscript, a 2008 study of African American women's perspectives on depression found that many "believed that an individual develops depression due to having a 'weak mind, poor health, a troubled spirit, and lack of self-love.'"

A member of the mental health profession currently working in higher education, Adrianne Traylor says, "I am cognizant of our community being left out of mental health discussions, not having appropriate access to mental health support, the cultural restrictions and barriers that keep us from seeking that support and that there are really not enough competent therapists to deal with situations that are unique to the Black experience in America. Finding a Black therapist to refer a client to is extremely difficult. Even when it comes to self-care, I think, 'Who am I going to talk to? Who am I going to refer myself to? Who can I talk to who can really understand what makes my situation unique as a Black woman?' We really lose out in the mental health equation—particularly when it comes to areas of depression, stress, and anxiety."[24]

Members of the Black community often learn that mental health care is something they neither need nor can afford—economically, socially, or culturally. Black folks are encouraged to take it to the Lord in prayer, but Adrianne stresses that many mental health issues cannot be ameliorated by a pastor, a friend, or family. Some mental illnesses require intensive therapy or psychotropic drugs, and not getting that treatment can be devastating.

Her own family provided her with a strong example of this cultural challenge. Adrianne says she grew up surrounded by women who exemplified the positive aspects of "Black women always being strong and resilient and always being able to carry everything." But as she grew older, "I saw the [unwillingness to pursue mental health care] weighing more heavily on the women in the family, because it seemed they were the ultimate repositories for sanity and intactness for everyone."

Moments in Alright

Nikki Myers credits a twelve-step program and yoga with saving her life from addiction. She founded Indianapolis's CITYOGA School of Yoga and Health and cofounded the Yoga of 12-Step Recovery (Y12SR) to help heal others. She has reached thousands around the world with her message of healing.[25]

When she was a teen, the house where Adrianne was born burned down. It was her grandmother's home and had been the center of many family memories. The loss was devastating to Adrianne. "But I remember watching [my grandmother], who was temporarily living in this itty-bitty house out in the country, and on the one hand admiring her strength. She had lost everything—her physical mementos of her life with her husband—everything. She seemed so strong and seemed on the surface to be coping. But I wondered what happened when she went to bed at night. What did she do then, when no one was looking at her? I started thinking if we were wearing a lot of masks to get through our lives and whether they were helping or hurting us.

"As you become older and more aware of family dysfunction... it is an awakening. You're oblivious to things as a kid and then your eyes open. You realize that the things that seemed like such strength could have really been someone doing what they could to hold things together."[26]

Thirty-five-year-old Vivian St. Claire* is a high achiever, perfectionist, and inveterate "good girl." She earned a PhD before she was thirty "because I was bored."[27]

Vivian also suffers from clinical depression. And three years ago, she had a nervous breakdown, driven in part by her relentless drive to meet societal expectations.

Despite her academic and professional success, Vivian couldn't shake the notion that she was a failure as a woman. A late bloomer in affairs of the heart, who was always more confident in intellectual pursuits than romantic ones, Vivian was childless and single, having just broken up with the man she once thought she would marry. "I never wanted to be the single Black woman, and I think that fear created that whole pressure."

Her undiagnosed clinical depression began to spiral out of control as Vivian grappled with fears about her personal life, her weight, and other issues. She began taking Ambien to cure the insomnia it caused—Ambien, red wine, and occasionally marijuana.

"I would black out," she says. "It was just all this very unhealthy mix of me trying to hide from a lot of different things. I know I was all over the place.

"Another part of my depression is I had a pact with myself: if I wasn't married by thirty-five, I was going to kill myself. I very much planned everything out for my life. At thirty-five, my plans ran out," she says. "That came out when I had my breakdown. My parents were in the room. While I was being evaluated, my mom was just sitting there silently crying.

"I would like to be more open with my struggle with depression—let close friends and things know," says Vivian. But she admits her openness is tempered with the realities of being an academic hoping for tenure and a desire not to "embarrass" her parents. Although they were there during her breakdown, they still have not processed her mental illness.

"My mom is fine with it for other people, but not her children—even though her brother is a paranoid schizophrenic." As her parents helped her complete paperwork that would commit her to the hospital, Vivian was surprised to hear her father answer in the affirmative when asked about mental illness on his side of the family.

"'Oh, yeah, your Auntie So-and-So has this. Your uncle is paranoid schizophrenic and whatever.'"

Black families often keep mental health histories under wraps, treating suffering members like guilty secrets. Quoting author Nalo Hopkinson in the book *Brown Girl in the Ring*, Vivian points out, "We as a people—our secrets are killing us."

It was a hard road back to mental health. Healing required that Vivian learn to be gentle with herself, to practice physical *and* mental self-care, to let go of her perfectionism, and to refuse to see her mental illness as a stigma.

"Today, I would say I'm the healthiest I've ever been—mentally and physically. I've come to a peace with myself. Yoga, therapy, being open about my mental illness and my medication, having coping mechanisms, and staying healthy—they are just part of my life now."

Her voice catches as she describes her pride at making it through: "At this point, every day it's a blessing that I'm happy, that I'm content with myself, and that I'm okay. I'm very proud of myself. I'm proud every day, because at least I keep holding on. It's not so much of a struggle for me anymore.

"Putting other people's pressure on me almost killed me. I've had to become comfortable with the uncomfortability of not being perfect. I'm amazed at the woman that I have become. . . . Sorry, I'm getting a little emotional, but it's been hard. It's been very hard. But I've earned a life beyond thirty-five years."

Chapter 8

Power
Fuck It, I'll Do It!

The 2018 national election brought more than twenty Black women to the United States Congress—a record number.[1] In 2020, America elected its first woman vice president. Kamala Harris is Black biracial, an HBCU grad and member of Alpha Kappa Alpha Sorority, Inc., one of the oldest Black Greek organizations.[2] Black women are leading a revolution in Dixie, turning Virginia and Georgia blue.[3] Three Black women founded Black Lives Matter, sowing the seeds for the modern civil rights movement. And the Me Too campaign against sexual violence and harassment—a Black woman started that, too.[4]

The treatment of these community activists, changemakers, and public servants is an example of how Black women are devalued and discounted, even as they labor for the greater good—how Jezebel, Sapphire, and Mammy can stalk Black women right into the halls of power and the front lines of revolution. But Black women's continued sacrifice and bold leadership demonstrates resilience and dedication to getting not just themselves free, but everybody.

How Black women wield power is a mirror to how they move in an unjust world.

"People Take One Look at Me and Dismiss Me"

For many Black women, their desire to use their power to help their communities comes from a deep well of empathy. They know how it feels to be unsupported and forgotten. They know that a society that treats humans this way is broken. And that people who benefit from the brokenness aren't likely to initiate repairs.

Halimah, thirty-eight, grew up in New York City, one of five kids raised by a mother living in poverty.[5] When her family struggled—and they often did—the only support available forced them into the system that has never valued Black life. Courts. Caseworkers. Foster care. Detention. Incarceration. At fourteen, Halimah committed a nonviolent offense and became a "juvenile lifer." "I came out [of detention] on my eighteenth birthday," she says.

Today, Halimah is an activist and servant leader. She advocates for Black families in the face of historic and systemic ambivalence. For instance, she has worked with the New York City Department of Health to address the startling maternal and infant mortality rate among Black women. But she quickly grows frustrated by foot-dragging and bureaucracy, and the thoughtless and violent tendency for government and NGOs to punish Black families they are purported to be helping.

"It took them five years to create the New York City standards for respectful care while birthing—a patient's bill of rights. Five years, because they [couldn't get the language right]. It should have taken five months," Halimah says. "[And we still] don't have anything to protect parents in case the medical institutions now want to involve these families in the child welfare system."

Halimah is passionate about getting Black families access to assistance that does not involve red tape and trauma. She is working as part of a participatory action research project with women and children who have been impacted by the child welfare system. It is designed to uncover what community support is available to families who look like the one she grew up in.

Halimah has also dedicated her life to being a source of community support, in big ways and small. She has supported and amplified birth workers in the Bronx.

"I used to work doing harm reduction, giving people syringes and providing condoms and lubricant and stuff like that," Halimah says. "We had good condoms—Magnums and Trojans... And I was like, 'I will bring some to my neighborhood.' Every night when I came home from work, I would just leave some on the mailboxes. I come out in the morning and everything is gone. I didn't even know until recently that, for over a year, I was known as the condom lady. People were like, 'Yeah, we know you—the lady that used to leave all of the condoms on the mailbox for people. Thank you for that!'"

During the COVID pandemic, she knocked on doors in her complex, making sure her neighbors were okay.

"I get frustrated about being in the hood," Halimah says. "I want to get the hell up outta here. I want to get my kids up out of here. But while I'm in the hood, I still make a difference."

All Black women are affected by racist and sexist stereotypes, but sisters who are poor, who live in underappreciated communities, who are single mothers, who have been justice involved—women like Halimah—bear an even heavier burden.

"I fight against it every day . . . all of the respectability politics. I'm Black. I'm still in the hood. I still swipe the EBT card. I guess I would be considered all of those stereotypes," she says. "Most of my life I've been told I don't belong in certain spaces—that I will never get to certain spaces acting in the way I do, looking the way I do and behaving the way that I do. I need to have all of these degrees and accolades in order to be accepted in certain spaces. People take one look at me and dismiss me."

But women like Halimah are often the backbones of their neighborhoods. They have the relationships, the drive, the knowledge, and the heart to offer real help to people who need it.

Lead like a Black Woman

Public service is a hereditary and cultural imperative for many Black women, born of communal values that stand in stark contrast to the "me first" ethos that is patriarchy. Black women work not just to get themselves free but to liberate everyone.

Jessica Louise, a thirty-something nonbinary femme activist who does liberation work in Indianapolis communities of color and is a core team member of Black Lives Matter in that city, says, "We have a greater sense of community. We find ways to care for others because that task has been passed to us. We've taken it and we've explored what it means to actually be in community with each other."[6]

She offers an example: "If I want to be free, that can mean something vastly different from a cis hetero, nuclear family that lives in the suburbs who consider their idea of freedom to be, you know, free from credit card or student loan debt. People deserve liberation and freedom in ways that make sense for them. My liberation cannot mean that I am harming or hurting other people.

Me being free means that I cannot give a vote to a law that is going to, say, impact a trans person."

Jessica adds, "If I don't speak up for someone who has accessibility needs, then that can also impact my freedom. People will see that we're allowing for violence to be done against those most marginalized groups and they'll just continue to notch it up until it comes to our door. We have to be vocal about the ills that are happening to our most marginalized people. We lend our social capital to their cause and make sure that they're not left behind and when it's time for liberation to come to our doors, we are actually ready for it."

The persistence of Mammy and Sapphire mythology makes the hard work of serving the community even harder. Black women often step forward to lead in freedom movements where they are still marginalized. Black women created the Black Lives Matter movement, but we still must plead to keep Black femme victims of police violence—like Atatiana Jefferson or Layleen Xtravaganza Cubilette-Polanco—from being forgotten.[7] Black women are allowed, even expected, to serve but not to have their lives (or deaths) centered. And not to lead. This is as frustratingly true in Black communities as it is in the larger political space.

Gender and racial politics have long obscured Black women's leadership in civil rights movements. Black men kept Black women, like movement organizer Dorothy Height, from speaking against the marginalization of Black people at the 1963 March on Washington.[8] White men obscured the importance of Marsha P. Johnson at the 1969 Stonewall Riots, where the Black trans woman was on the front line of people resisting a police raid on the gay bar.[9]

The strength it takes to serve the community is both doubted and demonized in Black women. Jessica has been organizing her whole life but still has to "bring my resume with me" to prove her ability to lead. "I've learned that when you come into the spaces that people are ready to give men the credit for things that they have only recently engaged in when these are things that you've been doing for 20 plus years."

And, she says, "There are a number of Black men in Indianapolis who . . . see our behavior as unladylike. And they figure that if we, um, if we operate outside of the confines of gender expression for Black women, then we deserve whatever happens to us. They celebrate when we're hurt. They celebrate. When things happen to us, they write about it. They convene about it. It is exhausting."

Service for Black women requires protecting themselves from the violence of the state and system. For instance, Bianca Mac, a thirty-six-year-old Portland organizer, was particularly vulnerable when she joined thousands of others in the streets to protest the police killings of George Floyd, Breonna Taylor, and others.[10] "I can't afford to go to jail. I don't want to run the risk of being imprisoned with men as a result of my being trans," she says. But it is an ugly truth that Black women activists and community organizers must also often protect themselves from some of the folks they are serving.

No one thanks the mule for pulling the plow or asks how she is feeling afterward. The looming picture of Black woman as Mammy explains why Jessica says, "[People] see our labor as something that should be given freely and unconditionally and without boundaries. We should not want credit for our labor. We should not want payment or compensation for our labor."

This was a common refrain from many Black woman public servants that I interviewed—that Black women are viewed as bottomless sources of service, requiring no thanks, acknowledgment, or assistance, no matter how monumental the task they face.

#ThankBlackWomen

But you would be forgiven for thinking, in the days after the 2020 presidential election, that Black women were finally getting their due. It took four soul-crushing days to officially know it, but United States senator Kamala Devi Harris (D-CA), a woman of Black and Asian descent, would be the new American vice president.[11] (Oh, and she was bringing Joseph Robinette Biden with her as president.)[12] After four terrifying years of White male supremacy violently asserting itself through a power-mad and feckless Republican Party led by an unhinged tyrant, it seemed Democracy was back.

And Black women were credited as the driving force behind it all.[13]

Nearly 91 percent of Black women voted for a Democratic presidency—a larger percentage than any other group.[14] That is as it always is. Black women habitually show up to do their civic duty and vote in their communities' best interests. But Black women were also on the front lines of work to block voter suppression, educate voters, and get them registered and to the polls to exercise their right to a voice in who governs them.

In 2018, Stacey Abrams lost her campaign for Georgia governor by just fifty-five thousand votes.[15] Over a decade, her opponent, Brian Kemp, who had been serving as Georgia's secretary of state, had purged 1.4 million people from voting rolls (some merely because they had missed voting in a previous election) and had overseen the institution of an "exact match" law that said handwritten voter registration must be identical to other personal documents. More than fifty-three thousand people—80 percent of them Black—had their voter registration temporarily held because of typos or minor mistakes.[16]

After her loss, Stacey Abrams, already the founder of New Georgia Project, a nonpartisan effort to register and civically engage Georgians, started "plotting." She founded Fair Fight, an organization devoted to voter rights, and got to work.[17] She wasn't alone. LaTosha Brown, cofounder of the Black Voters Matter Fund, had also been working to increase power in Black communities through voting.[18] Together, over two years, Abrams, Brown, and other voting rights activists—many of them Black women—registered more than eight hundred thousand new Georgia voters—nearly half of them under the age of thirty and/or people of color.[19] To the surprise of everyone who doesn't know to always bet on Black women, in 2020, Georgia turned "blue," delivering Senator Harris (and her running mate) to the White House and, after a runoff, two Democratic senators to Congress.[20]

For a time, media—traditional and social—erupted with appreciation. #ThankBlackWomen and #BlackWomenDidThis became trending hashtags. The *New York Times* said, "Georgia Was a Big Win for Democrats. Black Women Did the Groundwork."[21] Reuters Foundation published an article: "Black Women Voters Changed the Shape of the U.S. Election. It's Time to Thank Them."[22] Upworthy offered "15 Real Ways to Thank Black Women for Carrying the Country on Their Backs."[23]

All this adulation, though, was not necessarily a sign of society finally seeing Black women clearly or valuing their capability and strength. Indeed it made tokens of Black women—figureheads for the "woke" to reference for social currency. It did not dismantle the stereotypes that limit their humanity. It merely acknowledged that Black women, once again, had been forced to mediate with America's worst self on behalf of its better self and remind the country to breathe before it suffocates its own fool self.[24]

During her candidacy for the Democratic presidential nomination, Kamala Harris was accused of both sleeping her way to success (Jezebel) and being too aggressive in debates (Sapphire).[25] The Democratic electorate was generally tepid on the idea of a Black woman as a presidential nominee. But once Joe Biden won the 2020 primary, many people began lobbying for a Black woman to be his running mate.[26] Both Harris's and Abrams's names were discussed often. A Black woman could turn out the vote. A Black woman could energize young voters. A Black woman could bring about real reform. Perhaps more uncharitably: A Black woman could save America from the old, gaffe-prone White man voters chose to be their candidate instead of a Black woman.

Media thank-yous are nice enough. Better would be society supporting and valuing Black women not just when they give their labor on behalf of others, but also when they slip from the role of loyal helper to gaining power for their communities and themselves.

The Audacity of Black Women in Politics

In 2020, Dr. Adia Winfrey (no relation) was the Democratic candidate for the United States House of Representatives from Alabama's third district.[27] It was her second time as a candidate and the culmination of many years of community organizing and civic involvement. She had served as the chair of the party in Talladega County. And she was a critical factor in turning that county blue for former United States senator Doug Jones (D-AL), who served from 2018 until he was unseated in 2020 by Republican Tommy Tuberville.[28]

"My work began with organizing and I didn't even realize the value of it because, as a Black woman I was raised to be active in my community. It was just something I grew up doing, you know, knocking on doors, phone banking . . . I remember being a kid and working for campaigns. Those are things that win elections. [Black women] do these things for free. We're putting in these long hours. We are the reason why these people get into office."

Party officials who watched Adia harness community connections and turn out the vote were impressed, but their ardor waned for Adia the candidate. "When you try and get yourself elected, you're the enemy," she says. "It's like, 'How dare you put your name on the ballot?'"

Her campaign was such an afterthought that when, days before the 2020 election, officials held a state party event at a local college, they neglected to invite her. And though she had proved her mettle as a political asset supporting Doug Jones's 2018 election bid, even his campaign was silent. "No mentions, no value, no free stuff, no social media posts or retweets, no 'let's hop on Zoom together.'"

The experience was an eye opener. It made her reflect on Black women's political service. How too many people believe Black women are fit to follow but not to lead. "When it was Stacey Abrams running for governor of Georgia, they had all these reasons why she wasn't the one," Adia says. "It can't be them, you know? [Kamala Harris or Stacey Abrams]—they're both exemplary women. Harris wasn't my choice for president, but she was qualified."

Adia is proud of what she accomplished. "I was the first Black woman Congressional nominee in my district. So, we made history."

And she wants to stay in politics. The opportunity to make policy that improves the lives of her fellow citizens is worth the burden, she believes. Adia assembled an amazing, young, hard-working team for her congressional campaign. She is energized by what they might achieve together. Alabama could look like Georgia one day. She planned a meeting to strategize for the future before the 2020 election night was even over, because Adia is certain: America needs Black women.

"People don't realize they need us, but they do. Black women have always been the catalysts to moving this country forward," she says. "We are the PTO. We are the church. Whatever you want to name. We push everything and everybody is better because we push."

But she is going to move differently. And she thinks other Black women should, too.

Radical Self-Preservation

Adia suggests Black women unapologetically center their own needs in political and community work. "We have got to start being more selfish. We're doing it for them—the community and all that. And that is important. But we're doing it for us too."

And, she says, Black women must know their value and demand compensation for their work.

"Even when Black women are getting paid, the level of service that we're doing, what we're actually bringing is not matching up with the amount that we're getting paid. They use us up. Meanwhile, a lot of the people [on the payroll] are White."

She recently told a Democratic political operative looking to pick her brain, "Anything that y'all want to know about me, about my opinions and ideas for how to move forward, you will add me as a line item in your budget and send me a contract. Then we will talk. Black women have done enough for free. This Black woman will do nothing else."

Today's Black femme organizers and activists are learning what their foremothers also came to know. That, in the words of iconic feminist Audre Lorde, "Caring for myself is not self-indulgence, it is self-preservation, and that is an act of political warfare."

Few others will work to preserve the lives of Black women. This is another thing they must do for themselves.

"We have an obligation to look at Black women and femmes who have carried the labor of liberation forward and to recognize that they themselves might be burdened or in need of a break or in need of additional assistance," Jessica Louise adds. The bonds of sisterhood can lead Black women to watch out for each other—to see when another woman needs additional shoulders to carry a load. "Let me join up with you to relieve you . . . take some of this off of your plate so that you can then begin on your journey for healing and rest."[29]

Bianca believes that, because Black women are so present nurturing and caring for others, folks assume they spend equal effort tending to themselves and their sisters.[30] That isn't necessarily true. For Black women who do political and social justice work to be fully supported, other members of the community must learn the caretaking skills, too. It seems like a dangerous alternative if we don't: otherwise, we will continue to make Black women martyrs instead of humans with full and complex lives.

And Black women must prioritize their own rest, which is hard for women shaped by values and society to give of themselves.

Bianca is involved in mutual aid projects, where people take responsibility for caring for one another and changing political conditions. Sheltering in place during the coronavirus pandemic was difficult. There was still food to be delivered. Isolated people who needed a friendly word. But quarantine made some community work impossible.

"I can't say I'm resting, because I'm still so aware of what's going on," she says. "I still know where I'm not showing up. I still know where my capacity to do for something else is limited by spatial concerns, shelter in place concerns or resource concerns. Sometimes it's hard just knowing that there is nothing I can do [at the moment] for the betterment of my community."

But she has learned to embrace joy.

"One of my affirmations is celebrate our victories. Clearing my sink is a victory. Making a meal that I love is a victory. My car still starts when I need to go to the grocery store. That's a victory," Bianca says.

And there are bigger things, too. I interview Bianca on a special day—the anniversary of her transition. In the middle of the pandemic, sheltered in place, she was going to celebrate. Black women are wielding their power to make political and cultural change—to ensure communities and a country that remain ambivalent about them survive. But they are not made for the use of others. No human being is. Black women, who so frequently center others, need space to center themselves.

"I'm gonna put my favorite lipstick color on. I'm gonna pick a pretty dress. I'm gonna put on my shoes after neglecting to do that for a long time. It's a victory! Today is three years to the day that I answered the call on myself."

This is the dance Black women must do. We know, no matter what we give—have given—that society forgets our humanity. We don't forget. We know who we are. We know what we deserve. We know what our communities deserve. And so, we embrace our small joys. And we do the work. We do it around and despite misogynoir. And someday we will get ourselves free—and everybody else with us.

The Sisters Are Alright

Black women are not seeking special treatment—just to be treated as human beings of worth. We are looking for compassion. We are searching for good faith and the benefit of the doubt. We are hoping for relief from twisted images of ourselves and the burden of always having to first disprove what people think they know of us. If society will not give us this—if our communities will not demand this for us . . .

Black women will still be alright.

Collectively, we have troubles, yes—some very real and very serious, others the result of society's feverish imagination.

But we are alright.

Life is too short and too precious for us to be anything but.

"I'm alright, because I can't not be. It would cost me too much," says Bianca Mac, who transitioned during the hostile Trump presidency. "I know my worth and my value. I know what I'm capable of. I pull those things together and I make a person who is alright in the end."

"Tell them, as Troy Maxson told his son in August Wilson's *Fences*, 'Don't go through life worried about whether someone

likes you. You best be concerned that they do right by you,'"
preaches Deesha Philyaw.

"Let folks perceive you however they want—Jezebel, angry
Black woman, welfare queen—as long as they get the hell out of
the way and let you do your thing. Stop looking for approval and
permission from people who hate you and want to see you fail
and stop spending all your energy railing against their perceptions. Give yourself a daily/weekly/monthly allotment of outrage,
and then be about the business of building."

Let the church say "Amen."

Deesha feels strongly that systemic racism and sexism need
to be acknowledged and fought, but she adds that Black women
also need to be living as we are fighting.

"Raising conscious children, creating extraordinary art, getting the best revenge by living well in spite of racism and sexism.
If I spend all my time reacting, I can't act. I can't initiate and steer
the course of my life.

"Racism and sexism no longer hurt my feelings. I'm not
shocked by them. I'm not shocked that somebody thinks black-
face is hilarious or that dark-skinned girls are ugly. I know that
they are wrong, and instead of trying to convince them of anything, I just reaffirm what I know to be true by the stories I choose
to tell in my writing, by the kinds of dolls I buy for my children,
by my personal presentation, by what I put out into the world."

It seems that most Black women agree. Even as we worry
about paying our bills, maintaining our health, raising our children, keeping ourselves safe, and facing institutional biases, most
of us are happy to be exactly who we are. A 2012 nationwide survey by the *Washington Post* and the Kaiser Family Foundation
revealed that 67 percent of Black women say they have high self-
esteem. Eighty-five percent of us said we are satisfied with our

lives, and 73 percent say that now is a good time to be a Black woman.[1]

I asked several women why, despite tremendous pressure to feel differently, they are happy being Black women—I asked them how they achieved "alrightness."

"I'm alright," says Heather Carper, "because I understand human nature. [For so many people] to have spent so much time, effort, and expense to denigrate, defile, and destroy us, I know that my Black femaleness must be 'fearfully and wonderfully made' as the old church folks say. It cannot be bought. It cannot be imitated. And it cannot be destroyed."

Deesha says, "The racists and the sexists have failed miserably in trying to convince me that I don't matter, that I am less than. I spent the first thirty-five years of my life feeling that way, and not even because of racism or sexism. I decided that I didn't have any more time to waste living in fear of what other people thought of me, which really isn't living at all. Defining myself for myself and not giving that personal power away is what makes me alright. Not needing a racist or sexist person's permission for any fucking thing is what makes me alright. Not needing anyone to like me or approve of my politics or my aesthetic is what makes me alright. I have to be alright because I need my daughters to know that they are alright."

Jamyla Bennu says, "I am completely happy with my identity and it has never occurred to me not to be. I am in love with my Black woman self. I am in love with Black womanhood.

"I exalt in how many ways there are for us to be uniquely beautiful—the shapes and shades in which we walk the world. I love our laughter and fierceness and care and energy and exhaustion and brilliance and creativity. That perceptions other than this exist is honestly puzzling to me."

In a nod to literary great Zora Neale Hurston, Jamyla adds: "How could anyone deny themselves the pleasure of my company? It is beyond me."

Ebony Murphy-Root also quotes Sister Zora: "I love myself when I am laughing . . . and then again when I am looking mean and impressive."[2]

It is not surprising to hear Black women dropping wisdom from a famous foremother. From our earliest years, Black women draw strength and inspiration from our heritage and the women who came before us. We learn from them how to be okay, even when the world seems mad.

"I am my ancestors!" Morgan Overton says. "My being here is revolutionary within itself. My walk is a protest. [My foremothers] couldn't even have imagined a quarter of the things I have accomplished. I'm an embodiment of them. I know that I'm enough and that's what keeps me going. That's why I'm all right."

Fatima Thomas believes that although Black women are not unbreakable, we are "even at our lowest points, survivors. It's the small things for me that add up to who I am—something as simple as getting out of the bed when I'd rather ball up and cry for days. The fact that I *can* do that . . . the fact that with much less than I have . . . women who came before me and have this skin in common with me just kept getting up. The strong Black woman trope is a double-edged sword. As much as I want to just *be*, I actually am far stronger than most. I love that about us."

"We are alright because we recognize our worth as individuals and appreciate the knowledge that brought us into that space," Deborah Latham-White adds.

Our strength lies in the Black woman collective—past but also present. Jamyla encourages Black women to seek empowering relationships with other women and to make conscious decisions to support and nurture one another.

"We can change our personal narratives. I mean that in the way in which we tell our stories about ourselves to ourselves and to each other, the things we expect for ourselves."

While everyone whispers about our wrong, we can nod knowingly to each other and celebrate our right. When we are at our best, we practice this sisterhood across identities and experiences.

Bre Rivera, a trans sister, acknowledges that she is okay, in part "because there were cis women who were wise enough to actually, like, love on me, protect me and stand in the gap."

As a collective, we are something special—an unmatched force.

Halimah puts it succinctly, "Where would we be without us?"

Indeed.

What is wrong with Black women?

Simple answer: not a damned thing.

We're not perfect, but we're no more flawed than anyone else. In fact, most Black women believe it's pretty good to be us. We are not Jezebels or Mammies or Matriarchs or Sapphires. Or not just. Some of us are workhorses. Some of us are angry. Some of us are promiscuous. We are all and none of these things. Black women are human—with all the complexity that implies.

We have facets like diamonds. The trouble is the people who refuse to see us sparkling.

Notes

* Name changed at the request of the interviewee.

Preface

1. Rick Rojas et al., "'A Long Time Coming': Black Women Celebrate Harris's Ascension," *New York Times*, November 8, 2020, https://www.nytimes.com /2020/11/07/us/kamala-harris-black-women-first.html.

2. Marwa Eltagouri, "Meet Andrea Jenkins, the First Openly Transgender Black Woman Elected to Public Office in the U.S.," *Washington Post*, April 28, 2019, https://www.washingtonpost.com/news/the-fix/wp/2017/11/08/meet-andrea -jenkins-the-openly-transgender-black-woman-elected-to-public-office-in -the-u-s/.

3. Sony Salzman, "From the Start, Black Lives Matter Has Been about LGBTQ Lives," ABC News, June 21, 2020, https://abcnews.go.com/US/start-black-lives -matter-lgbtq-lives/story?id=71320450.

4. Ruth Umoh, "Black Women Were among the Fastest-Growing Entrepreneurs— Then Covid Arrived," *Forbes*, October 26, 2020, https://www.forbes.com/sites /ruthumoh/2020/10/26/black-women-were-among-the-fastest-growing -entrepreneurs-then-covid-arrived/?sh=407d83c66e01.

5. Sarah Rufca Nelson, "The 6 Buzziest Times Beyoncé Broke the Internet," *Houstonia*, August 15, 2019, https://www.houstoniamag.com/arts-and-culture /2017/06/beyonce-breaking-the-internet.

6. Emily Steel and Michael S. Schmidt, "Bill O'Reilly Settled New Harassment Claim, Then Fox Renewed His Contract," *New York Times*, October 21, 2017, https://www.nytimes.com/2017/10/21/business/media/bill-oreilly-sexual -harassment.html.

7. "About #SAY HER NAME," African American Policy Forum, 2014, https:// www.aapf.org/sayhername.

8. Grace Carroll, "Snoop Dogg Claims He 'Sold' Women to Fellow Stars While on Tour," Gigwise, May 9, 2013, https://www.gigwise.com/news/81484/; Natasha Jokic, "Snoop Dogg Made a Bunch of Sexist Comments about 'WAP,' and Offset Responded," BuzzFeed, December 17, 2020, https://www.buzzfeed.com /natashajokic1/snoop-dogg-wap-controversy; Alisha Haridasani Gupta, "Why Aren't We All Talking about Breonna Taylor?," *New York Times*, June 4, 2020, https://www.nytimes.com/2020/06/04/us/breonna-taylor-black-lives-matter -women.html; Linda Villarosa, "Why America's Black Mothers and Babies Are in a Life-or-Death Crisis," *New York Times*, April 11, 2018, https://www.nytimes .com/2018/04/11/magazine/black-mothers-babies-death-maternal-mortality .html; John Eligon, "Black Doctor Dies of Covid-19 after Complaining of Racist Treatment," *New York Times*, December 24, 2020, https://www.nytimes.com /2020/12/23/us/susan-moore-black-doctor-indiana.html.

9. "3 Questions: Moya Bailey on the Intersection of Racism and Sexism," Program in Women's and Gender Studies, MIT News, January 11, 2021, https://news.mit .edu/2021/3-questions-moya-bailey-intersection-racism-sexism-0111.

Introduction: The Trouble with Black Women

1. Bill Johnson, "Opinion: Aretha Franklin Eulogy Was True. Single-Parent Homes Created Chaos for Blacks," Bridge Michigan, September 11, 2018, https:// www.bridgemi.com/guest-commentary/opinion-aretha-franklin-eulogy -was-true-single-parent-homes-created-chaos-blacks.

2. "Why Can't a Successful Black Woman Find a Man?," ABC News, March 26, 2010, https://abcnews.go.com/Nightline/successful-black-woman-find-man /story?id=10213505.

3. Noah Berlatsky, "Beyoncé, Sex Terrorist: A Menace for Conservatives and Liberals Alike," *Atlantic*, May 12, 2014, http://www.theatlantic.com /entertainment/archive/2014/05/beyonce-sex-terrorist-a-menace-for -conservatives-and-liberals-alike/362085/.

4. Akiba Solomon, "The Pseudoscience of 'Black Women Are Less Attractive,'" Colorlines, Race Forward, April 18, 2015, https://www.colorlines.com/articles /pseudoscience-black-women-are-less-attractive; Philiana Ng, "Oscars: The Onion Under Fire for Calling Quvenzhane Wallis the C-Word," *Hollywood Reporter*, February 25, 2013, http://www.hollywoodreporter.com/news/onion -calls-quvenzhane-wallis-c-424113.

5. Antonia Blumberg, "WATCH: Women Respond to Pastor's Sermon 'These Hoes Ain't Loyal,'" *HuffPost*, June 6, 2014, https://www.huffpost.com/entry /-jamal-bryant-hoes-aint-loyal_n_5459930.

6. Brande Victorian, "Tyrese to Black Women: 'You're Going to Independent Your Way into Loneliness,'" MadameNoire, November 14, 2011, https://madamenoire .com/90435/tyrese-to-womenyoure-going-to-independent-your-way-into -loneliness/.

7. Keli Goff, "Why Black Women Should Not Forgive Kevin Hart Even If Ellen Does (Guest Column)," *Hollywood Reporter*, January 7, 2019, https://www .hollywoodreporter.com/news/why-black-women-should-not-forgive-kevin -hart-ellen-does-guest-column-1173410.

8. "D.L. Hughley: Tough Words on Politics and Women," *Tell Me More*, NPR, October 25, 2012, https://www.npr.org/2012/10/25/163628656/d-l-hughley -tough-words-on-politics-and-women.

9. Michael Schneider, "Kenan Thompson Is Already an 'SNL' Legend, but Now He's Ready and Overdue for More," *Variety*, February 10, 2021, https://variety .com/2021/tv/news/kenan-thompson-saturday-night-live-snl-1234903357/.

10. Evan Hill et al., "How George Floyd Was Killed in Police Custody," *New York Times*, June 1, 2020, https://www.nytimes.com/2020/05/31/us/george-floyd -investigation.html.

11. Eliott C. McLaughlin, "An Officer Was Indicted for Endangering Neighbors, but Not Breonna Taylor, with His Bullets. This May Be Why," CNN, October 1, 2020, https://www.cnn.com/2020/10/01/us/legal-analysis-breonna-taylor -grand-jury/index.html.

12. Rebecca L. Spang, "The Revolution Is Under Way Already," *Atlantic*, April 5, 2020, https://www.theatlantic.com/ideas/archive/2020/04/revolution-only-getting-started/609463/.

13. "I Like That," MP3 audio, on Janelle Monáe, *Dirty Computer*, Wondaland Studios, Atlanta, GA, Organized Noize, 2018.

14. Jazmin Duribe, "Khloe Kardashian Is Being Roasted for 'Cosplaying' as Beyoncé and the Memes Are Brutal," PopBuzz, September 30, 2020, https://www.popbuzz.com/internet/viral/khloe-kardashian-beyonce-new-face-memes/.

15. Dade Hayes, "Gayle King Rips CBS for Excerpting Her Lisa Leslie Interview about Kobe Bryant; Network Responds—Update," Deadline, February 6, 2020, https://deadline.com/2020/02/gayle-king-kobe-bryant-cbs-news-lisa-leslie-1202853069/.

16. Jael Goldfine, "Snoop Dogg Comes for Gayle King, Oprah over Kobe Bryant," *Paper*, June 15, 2020, https://www.papermag.com/snoop-dogg-gayle-king-oprah-kobe-2645056676.html.

17. Doha Madani, "Snoop Dogg Apologizes to Gayle King for Attack over Kobe Bryant Sexual Assault Question," NBCNews.com, February 13, 2020, https://www.nbcnews.com/pop-culture/pop-culture-news/snoop-dogg-apologizes-gayle-king-attack-over-kobe-bryant-sexual-n1136151.

18. Kenya Evelyn, "Black US Authors Top New York Times Bestseller List as Protests Continue," *Guardian*, June 11, 2020, https://www.theguardian.com/books/2020/jun/11/new-york-times-bestseller-list-black-authors.

19. Royce Dunmore, "'Free Bill Cosby': Snoop Dogg Capes for Black Men While Slamming Oprah and Gayle King," NewsOne, March 31, 2020, https://newsone.com/3901694/bill-cosby-snoop-dogg-capes-black-men-oprah-and-gayle-king/.

20. Pearl K. Dowe, "Kamala Harris and the Stereotypes We Place on Black Women," *The Hill*, October 13, 2020, https://thehill.com/opinion/campaign/520884-kamala-harris-and-the-stereotypes-we-place-on-black-women.

21. Patricia Hill Collins, *Black Feminist Thought: Knowledge, Consciousness, and the Politics of Empowerment*, 2nd ed. (New York: Routledge, 2000), 79.

22. Claire Jean Kim, "The Racial Triangulation of Asian Americans," SAGE Journals, March 1, 1999, https://journals.sagepub.com/doi/abs/10.1177/0032329299027001005.

23. Kim, "Racial Triangulation," 80.

24. Kim, 81.

25. C. M. West, "Mammy, Jezebel, Sapphire, and Their Homegirls: Developing an 'Oppositional Gaze' toward the Images of Black Women," in *Lectures on the Psychology of Women*, ed. J. Chrisler, C. Golden, and P. Rozee, 4th ed. (New York: McGraw Hill, 2008), 289.

26. West, "Mammy, Jezebel, Sapphire," 289.

27. Collins, *Black Feminist Thought*, 81.

28. Collins, 80.

29. West, "Mammy, Jezebel, Sapphire," 290.

30. West, 290.

31. West, 290.

32. West, 294.

33. Collins, *Black Feminist Thought*, 91.

34. Collins, 83.

35. Office of Policy Planning and Research, United States Department of Labor, *The Negro Family: The Case for National Action* (Washington, DC: 1965).

36. Collins, *Black Feminist Thought*, 83.

37. Sheilla Mamona, "This Is Why, as a Black Woman, Being Called a Bully like Meghan Markle Is Triggering," *Glamour* UK, March 8, 2021, https://www .glamourmagazine.co.uk/article/meghan-markle-racism-lessons; Gerrard Kaonga, "Meghan Markle Accused of 'Humiliating and Manipulating' Prince Harry with 2020 Antics," Express.co.uk, January 2, 2021, https://www.express .co.uk/news/royal/1378891/Meghan-Markle-Prince-Harry-Duke-Duchess-Sussex -2020-news-latest-update-vn; Samantha Schnurr, "Here's the Shocking Advice Meghan Markle Was Given as a New Royal: 'Be 50 Percent Less,'" E! Online, March 8, 2021, https://www.eonline.com/news/1245710/heres-the-shocking -advice-meghan-markle-was-given-as-a-new-royal-be-50-percent-less.

38. Tamara Winfrey-Harris, "No Disrespect: Black Women and the Burden of Respectability," *Bitch*, Summer 2021, 32–37.

39. Winfrey-Harris, "No Disrespect."

40. Winfrey-Harris, "No Disrespect."

41. Sarah J. Jackson, interview by author, phone, November 2, 2012.

42. Ameena Hester, "What You Don't Learn about Sojourner Truth: 3 Things to Know," YR Media, February 18, 2021, https://yr.media/news/what-you-dont -learn-about-sojourner-truth-3-things-to-know/. From the article:

> The popularized version of Truth's speech, entitled "Ain't I a Woman?" is but a "faint sketch" of Truth's original speech according to historians, and is attributed to the white abolitionist Francis Dana Barker Gage. Gage published the altered speech 12 years after it was originally delivered, amending all the words and curtailing Truth's authentic voice.
>
> Sojourner Truth was of Dutch descent and spoke a now-extinct, low-Dutch dialect of English. Gage's version wrongly associates Truth, a Northerner, with Southern slave culture and its negative connotations. Whether intentional or unintentional, the amended speech perpetuates vernacular stereotypes of Black Southerners and grossly alienates enslaved people from cultural nuance. Even as a freed woman, Truth was victim to these parallels.
>
> Sojourner Truth, "Ain't I a Woman," address at Women's Convention, Akron, Ohio, May 29, 1851, http://www.feminist.com/resources/artspeech /genwom/sojour.htm.

43. West, "Mammy, Jezebel, Sapphire," 287.

44. Melissa V. Harris-Perry, *Sister Citizen* (New Haven: Yale University Press, 2011), 29.

45. Kawana, interview by author, online, July 24, 2014.

46. Wendi Muse, interview by author, phone, August 31, 2014.

47. Alexandra Cawthorne, "The Straight Facts on Women in Poverty," Center for American Progress, October 8, 2008.

48. US Department of Health and Human Services and National Institutes of Health, *The Heart Truth for Women*, NIH Publication No. 07-5066 (Washington, DC: originally printed September 2003, revised July 2009).

49. US Census Bureau, "2010 US Census Marital Status Chart," table 57: "Marital Status of the Population by Sex and Age," accessed December 27, 2011.

50. *Women of Color Network Facts & Stats: Domestic Violence in Communities of Color*, Women of Color Network (Harrisburg, PA: June 2006), http://www.doj.state .or.us/wp-content/uploads/2017/08/women_of_color_network_facts_domestic _violence_2006.pdf.

51. Derek Thompson, "The Workforce Is Even More Divided by Race Than You Think," *Atlantic*, November 13, 2013, https://www.theatlantic.com/business /archive/2013/11/the-workforce-is-even-more-divided-by-race-than-you -think/281175/.

52. Lisa Myers Bulmash, interview by author, phone, March 24, 2012.

53. Nichelle Hayes, interview by author, July 2, 2014.

Chapter 1: Beauty: Pretty for a Black Girl

1. Brittney Oliver, "Boss Moves: Inside Rihanna's Business Queendom," *Essence*, February 20, 2021, https://www.essence.com/celebrity/boss-moves-inside -rihanna-business-queendom/; "How Fenty Revolutionized the Beauty Industry," *Vogue Paris*, May 29, 2019, https://www.vogue.fr/beauty-tips/article/how-fenty -revolutionized-the-beauty-industry.

2. Patrice Grell Yursik, interview by author, December 29, 2020.

3. Oliver, "Boss Moves."

4. Lois Sakany, "Rihanna Provides First Look at Fenty Beauty with Campaign Ft. Halima Aden, Slick Woods & More," Snobette, December 3, 2017, https:// snobette.com/2017/09/rihanna-introduces-fenty-beauty-campaign-slick-woods -halima-aden-duckie-thot/.

5. Franchesca Ramsey, "Makeup Artists Rarely Have Foundation for This Black Model. In 2015, There's No Excuse," Upworthy, May 31, 2019, https://www .upworthy.com/makeup-artists-rarely-have-foundation-for-this-black-model-in -2015-theres-no-excuse.

6. "Famous Feminist Quotes That Keep Fuelling the Debate," *Telegraph*, September 21, 2015, https://www.telegraph.co.uk/film/suffragette/famous_feminist _quotes/.

7. Bre Rivera, interview by author, January 15, 2021.

8. Heather Carper, interview by author, August 13, 2014.

9. Thomas Jefferson, *Notes on the State of Virginia*, ed. William Peden (Chapel Hill: University of North Carolina Press for the Institute of Early American History and Culture, Williamsburg, Virginia, 1954).

10. Patricia Hill Collins, *Black Feminist Thought: Knowledge, Consciousness, and the Politics of Empowerment*, 2nd ed. (New York: Routledge, 2000), 98.

11. Khadijah Britton, "The Data Are in Regarding Satoshi Kanazawa," Scientific American Blog Network, *Scientific American*, May 23, 2011, https://blogs .scientificamerican.com/guest-blog/the-data-are-in-regarding-satoshi-kanazawa/.

12. Dahvi Shira, "Anala Beevers Is a 4-Year-Old Genius," *People*, July 27, 2013, https://people.com/celebrity/anala-beevers-is-a-4-year-old-genius/.

13. Karen Grigsby Bates, "At Fashion Week, Color Pops and Models Call for Diversity," NPR, September 14, 2013, https://www.npr.org/sections /codeswitch/2013/09/13/222170186/at-fashion-week-color-pops-and-models -call-for-diversity.

14. Cordelia Tai, "Report: Racial, Size and Gender Diversity Get a Boost at New York Fashion Week Spring 2020," The Fashion Spot, September 30, 2019, https://www.thefashionspot.com/runway-news/846053-diversity-report-new -york-fashion-week-spring-2020/.

15. Black Witch, interview by author, September 17, 2014.

16. Liz Hurston, interview by author, phone, August 17, 2014.

17. A. Springer, "Kanye West Calls Mixed Girls 'Mutts,'" HipHopDX, December 2, 2006, https://hiphopdx.com/news/id.4685/title. kanye-west-calls-mixed-girls-mutts#signup.

18. Jon Blistein, "Kanye West Concedes Self-Serving Presidential Bid, Threatens 2024 Run," *Rolling Stone*, November 5, 2020, https://www.rollingstone.com /music/music-news/kanye-west-2020-presidential-run-votes-election-1086059/.

19. Wanna Thompson, "White Women on Instagram Are Successfully Posing as Black Women," *Paper*, June 15, 2020, https://www.papermag.com/white-women -blackfishing-instagram-2619714094.html.

20. Jazmin Duribe, "Khloe Kardashian Is Being Roasted for 'Cosplaying' as Beyoncé and the Memes Are Brutal," PopBuzz, September 30, 2020, https://www .popbuzz.com/internet/viral/khloe-kardashian-beyonce-new-face-memes/.

21. "A Look Back at the Kardashian Family's Humble Armenian Roots," *People*, April 10, 2015, https://people.com/celebrity/a-look-back-at-the-kardashian -familys-humble-armenian-roots/.

22. Thompson, "White Women on Instagram."

23. Erin Millender, interview by author, August 20, 2014.

24. "Rutgers Players Describe How Imus' Remarks Hurt," CNN, April 10, 2007, http://www.cnn.com/2007/SHOWBIZ/TV/04/10/imus.rutgers/index.html.

25. Moe, "'Glamour' Editor to Lady Lawyers: Being Black Is Kinda a Corporate 'Don't,'" Jezebel, August 14, 2007, http://jezebel.com/289268/glamour-editor -to-lady-lawyers-being-Black-is-kinda-a-corporate-don't.

26. Karen Grigsby Bates, "Congressional Black Caucus Urges Rethink of Army Hair Rules," NPR, April 11, 2014, http://www.npr.org/blogs/codeswitch/2014 /04/11/301509842/congressional-Black-caucus-urges-rethink-of-army-hair -rules.

27. Victoria M. Massie, "Federal Appeals Court Rules It's Okay to Discriminate against Black Hairstyles like Dreadlocks," Vox, September 19, 2016, https:// www.vox.com/2016/9/19/12971790/court-discriminate-dreadlocks.

28. "Second-Grader's Dreadlocks Cause for Concern?," *Tell Me More*, NPR, September 12, 2013, https://www.npr.org/2013/09/12/221738347/second-graders -dreadlocks-cause-for-concern.

29. Dominique Hobdy, "School Threatens to Expel Girl for Wearing Hair Natural," *Essence*, November 26, 2013, https://www.essence.com/news/florida-school -threatens-expel-african-american-girl-wearing-natural-hair/.

30. Michelle Hunter, "After Hair Extensions Ban and Viral Video, New Orleans-Area School Faces Civil Rights Lawsuit," NOLA.com, *Times-Picayune* and *New Orleans Advocate*, August 8, 2019, https://www.nola.com/news/courts/article _415be8f8-ba1d-11e9-a55b-5752e61a2fea.html.

31. Patrice Grell Yursik, interview by author, August 15, 2014.

32. Felicia Leatherwood, interview by author, August 19, 2014.

33. Felicia Leatherwood interview.

34. Jamyla Bennu, interview by author, September 7, 2014.

35. Tonya Garcia, "L'Oreal USA Purchases Carol's Daughter to Reach the Multicultural Market," Madame Noire, October 20, 2014, http://madamenoire.com /480079/loreal-usa-purchases-carols-daughter-to-reach-the-multicultural -market/.

36. Felicia Leatherwood interview.

37. Heben Nigatu, "Teyonah Parris Has the Flyest Hair on the Red Carpet," Buzzfeed, April 10, 2014, http://www.buzzfeed.com/hnigatu/ teyonah-parris-has-the-flyest-hair-on-the-red-carpet.

38. Chanel Parks, "Teyonah Parris Cried over Her Natural Hair: It Didn't Look like 'What I Thought Was Beautiful,'" *Huffington Post*, July 15, 2014, http://www .huffingtonpost.com/2014/07/15/teyonah-parris-natural-hair_n_5587721.html.

39. Philip Bump, "The Most Likely Person to Read a Book? A College-Educated Black Woman," *Atlantic*, January 16, 2014, https://www.theatlantic.com/culture /archive/2014/01/most-likely-person-read-book-college-educated-black-woman /357091/.

40. Patrice Grell Yursik interview.

41. Heather Carper interview.

42. Patrice Grell Yursik interview.

Chapter 2: Sex: Wet-Ass Pussy

1. "Anaconda," MP3 audio single, from Nicki Minaj, *The Pinkprint*, produced by Da Internz, AnonXmous, Polow da Don, Glenwood Recording Studios, Burbank, CA, 2014.

2. "Rules," on Doja Cat, *Hot Pink*, produced by Dr. Luke, Salaam Remi, and Ben Billions, eightysevenfourteen studios, Los Angeles, CA, 2019, CD.

3. Nicki Minaj often refers to other women rappers as her "sons." According to an Urban Dictionary entry by Cirocwave on March 11, 2011, the phrase means Nicki birthed the other rap stars and she's showing them how it's done.

4. "About," Women of Color Sexual Health Network, http://www.wocshn.org/about/.

5. Rachel Holmes, *African Queen: The Real Life of the Hottentot Venus* (New York: Random House, 2007), loc. 66 of 2679.

6. Sean Carroll, "Venus Hottentot and the Irony of Science," *Discover*, December 22, 2008, https://www.discovermagazine.com/the-sciences/venus-hottentot -and-the-irony-of-science.

7. Holmes, *African Queen*, loc. 1664 of 2679.

8. "Regis Philbin Hits on Nicki Minaj," Daily Beast, January 1, 2011, video, http:// www.thedailybeast.com/videos/2011/01/18/regis-philbin-hits-on-nicki-minaj.html.

9. Jared Keller, "LAPD Confuses Black Actress Kissing White Partner for Prostitute," Mic, September 13, 2014, https://www.mic.com/articles/98826/lapd-confuses-black-actress-kissing-white-partner-for-prostitute.

10. C. M. West, "Mammy, Jezebel, Sapphire, and Their Homegirls: Developing an 'Oppositional Gaze' toward the Images of Black Women," in *Lectures on the Psychology of Women*, ed. J. Chrisler, C. Golden, and P. Rozee, 4th ed. (New York: McGraw Hill, 2008), 2.

11. Odia Kane, "The Denial of Black Victimhood: Examining Attitudes of Sexual Assault and Victim-Blaming on a College Campus, A Continued Analysis" (master's thesis, University of Connecticut, 2020), 1507, https://opencommons.uconn.edu/gs_theses/1507.

12. Catherine Taibi, "Here's the One Question Bill O'Reilly Is Dying to Ask Beyonce," *Huffington Post*, March 16, 2014, http://www.huffingtonpost.com/2014/03/16/bill-oreilly-beyonce-letterman-thug-show-fox_n_4974574.html.

13. Allie Jones, "Bill O'Reilly Blames Beyoncé for Black Teen Pregnancy," *Atlantic*, April 29, 2014, https://www.theatlantic.com/politics/archive/2014/04/bill-oreilly-blames-beyonce-for-black-teen-pregnancy/361385/.

14. Taibi, "Here's the One Question."

15. Megan Garber, "Why Was Bill O'Reilly Really Fired?" *Atlantic*, April 19, 2017, https://www.theatlantic.com/news/archive/2017/04/why-was-bill-oreilly-really-fired/523614/.

16. Kathryn Kost and Stanley Henshaw, *U.S. Teenage Pregnancies, Births and Abortions, 2010: National and State Trends by Age, Race and Ethnicity* (New York: Guttmacher Institute, 2014).

17. Tamara Winfrey-Harris, "All Hail the Queen?," *Bitch*, Summer 2013, http://bitchmagazine.org/article/all-hail-the-queen-beyonce-feminism.

18. "Awards & Honors," "Boards & Steering Committees," Bio, Tamika Felder, accessed April 27, 2021, https://www.tamikafelder.com/bio/.

19. Hadley Freeman, "Beyoncé: Being Photographed in Your Underwear Doesn't Help Feminism," *Guardian*, January 15, 2013, http://www.theguardian.com/commentisfree/2013/jan/15/beyonce-photographed-underwear-feminism.

20. See Anne Helen Petersen, *Celebrity Gossip, Academic Style* (blog), Facebook, https://www.facebook.com/pages/Celebrity-Gossip-Academic-Style/180012152012326.

21. Quoted from a reply to Dodai Stewart, "Beyoncé's 'Documentary' Was Just a Theatrical Infomercial," Jezebel, February 18, 2013, http://jezebel.com/5985033/beyonces-documentary-was-just-a-theatrical-infomercial.

22. Nojma Muhammad, "Nicki Minaj AKA 'Miss HottenTHOT,'" Thy Black Man, August 21, 2014, http://thyBlackman.com/2014/08/21/nicki-minaj-aka-miss-hottenthot/.

23. Muhammad, "Nicki Minaj."

24. "BET CEO Debra Lee Speaks on Banning Degrading Music Videos and Positive Change at BET Networks," Z107.9 (website), June 19, 2019, https://zhiphopcleveland.com/2831621/bet-ceo-debra-lee-speaks-on-banning-degrading-music-videos-positive-change-at-bet-networks/.

25. Cristal Lee, interview by author, June 30, 2014.

26. Bianca Giacabone, "In New York, Burlesque Meets the Feminist Struggle," the Submarine, October 27, 2020, https://thesubmarine.it/2020/10/22/burlesque-feminist-struggle/.

27. "WAP," CD single, recorded by Cardi B, featuring vocals from Megan Thee Stallion, from Cardi B, featuring Megan Thee Stallion, *WAP*, produced by Ayo the Producer and Keyz, Atlantic Records, 2020.

28. "Girls in the Hood," on Megan Thee Stallion, *Good News*, produced by IllaDa-Producer et al., 1501 Certified and 300 Entertainment, 2020, CD.

29. "I Do," on Cardi B, *Invasion of Privacy*, produced by CuBeatz et al., Atlantic, 2018, CD.

30. Angelica Florio, "Janelle Monáe's New Video about Female Sexuality Will Leave You Feeling like a Goddess," Bustle, April 10, 2018, https://www.bustle.com/p/janelle-monaes-pynk-video-about-female-sexuality-will-make-you-feel-like-a-goddess-8746306.

31. Megan Thee Stallion, "Megan Thee Stallion: Why I Speak Up for Black Women," *New York Times*, October 13, 2020, https://www.nytimes.com/2020/10/13/opinion/megan-thee-stallion-black-women.html.

32. Kai Chapman, interview by author, December 29, 2020.

33. "Some Cut," CD single, from Trillville, *The King of Crunk & BME Present: Trillville & Lil Scrappy*, produced by Lil Jon, Warner Bros. Records, 2004.

34. Goddess Honey, interview by author, December 24, 2020.

35. "The New Sexual Revolution: Polyamory on the Rise," *1A*, NPR, February 18, 2019, https://www.npr.org/2019/02/18/695731314/the-new-sexual-revolution-polyamory-on-the-rise-listen.

36. Yael Malka, Alice Hines, and Eve Lyons, "Polyamory Works for Them," *New York Times*, August 3, 2019, https://www.nytimes.com/2019/08/03/style/polyamory-nonmonogamy-relationships.html.

37. Sarah Thomas, "Black Women Face Greater Scrutiny than White Women for Being Polyamorous," The Black Youth Project, December 20, 2019, http://blackyouthproject.com/black-women-face-greater-scrutiny-than-white-women-for-being-polyamorous/.

38. Andrea Plaid, interview by author, August 20, 2014.

Chapter 3: Marriage: Witches, Thornbacks, and Sapphires

1. Erica Johnson, interview by author, May 25, 2012.

2. Ralph Richard Banks, *Is Marriage for White People? How the African American Marriage Decline Affects Everyone* (New York: Dutton, 2011), 7.

3. Kerry Hannon, "Black Women Entrepreneurs: The Good and Not-So-Good News," *Forbes*, September 9, 2018, https://www.forbes.com/sites/nextavenue/2018/09/09/black-women-entrepreneurs-the-good-and-not-so-good-news/?sh=13ae0abe6ffe.

4. D'Vera Cohn et al., "Barely Half of U.S. Adults Are Married—A Record Low," Pew Research Social & Demographics Trends, Pew Research Center,

December 14, 2011, http://www.pewsocialtrends.org/2011/12/14/barely-half-of
-u-s-adults-are-married-a-record-low/.

5. "The State of American Households: Smaller, More Diverse and Unmarried,"
   U.S. News & World Report, February 14, 2020, https://www.usnews.com/news
   /elections/articles/2020-02-14/the-state-of-american-households-smaller-more
   -diverse-and-unmarried#:~:text=In%201990%2C%2043%25%20of%20
   black,2019%2C%20it%20was%2051%25.

6. "The State of American Households," *U.S. News & World Report*.

7. George Bernard Shaw, *Man and Superman. A Comedy and a Philosophy* (Cam-
   bridge, MA: University Press, 1903).

8. Julie Coleman, *Love, Sex, and Marriage: A Historical Thesaurus* (Amsterdam:
   Costerus, 1999).

9. Kate Constance, "A Check List on Marriage Rating," *Kansas City Star*, September 25, 1957, reprinted on The Retro Housewife, http://www.retro-housewife
   .com/1957-check-list-on-marriage-rating.html (site discontinued).

10. Michiko Kakutani, "Women as Witches," Books of the Times, *New York Times*,
    November 21, 1987, http://www.nytimes.com/1987/11/21/books/books-of-the
    -times-women-as-witches.html.

11. Katherine Boo, "The Marriage Cure: Is Wedlock Really a Way Out of Poverty?,"
    New Yorker, April 18, 2003, http://www.newyorker.com/magazine/2003/08/18
    /the-marriage-cure.

12. Steve Harvey and Denene Millner, *Act like a Lady, Think like a Man* (New York:
    Amistad, 2009), 182.

13. Harvey and Millner, *Act like a Lady*, 180.

14. Carolyn Edgar, interview by author, June 2, 2012.

15. Cherrie Moraga and Gloria Anzaldua, "Lesbianism as Resistance" (essay), in
    This Bridge Called My Back: Writings by Radical Women of Color (Albany, NY: State
    University of New York Press, 1981), 128.

16. Nichelle Hayes, interview by author, June 12, 2014.

17. US Census Bureau, "2010 Annual Social and Economic Supplement," Current
    Population Survey, internet release date: November 2010.

18. D. Henry, interview by author, June 3, 2012.

19. *Black Women in the United States, 2014*, National Coalition on Black Civic
    Participation and Black Women's Roundtable, vii.

20. Gretchen Livingston and Anna Brown, "1. Trends and Patterns in Intermar-
    riage," Pew Research Center's Social & Demographic Trends Project, Pew
    Research Center, May 30, 2020, https://www.pewresearch.org/social-trends
    /2017/05/18/1-trends-and-patterns-in-intermarriage/.

21. Allison P. Davis, "New OKCupid Data on Race Is Pretty Depressing," The Cut,
    September 11, 2014, https://www.thecut.com/2014/09/new-okcupid-data-on
    -race-is-pretty-depressing.html.

22. Tiffany Allen-White and Trayvia Allen-White, interview by author, January 30, 2021.

23. Sharon Jayson, "Free as a Bird and Loving It: Being Single Has Its Benefits,"
    USA Today, April 12, 2007, http://usatoday30.usatoday.com/news/health/2007
    -04-11-being-single_n.htm.

24. Kim Akins, interview by author, March 18, 2012.

Chapter 4: Motherhood: Between Mammy and a Hard Place

1. Lisa Belkin, "Michelle Obama: What Does She Mean by 'Mom in Chief'?," *Huffington Post*, September 5, 2012, http://www.huffingtonpost.com/lisa-belkin /obama-mom-in-chief_b_1858440.html.

2. Libby Copeland, "Why Are Presidential Candidates' Wives All the Same?," *Slate*, September 7, 2012, http://www.slate.com/articles/double_x/doublex /2012/09/first_wives_club_why_are_presidential_candidates_spouses_all_the _same_.html.

3. Sadie Whitelocks, "Black Women Pushing White Babies: Photo Series Exposes the Racial Divides in the World of a NY Nanny," *Daily Mail*, January 15, 2014, http://www.dailymail.co.uk/femail/article-2540015/Black-women-pushing -white-babies-Candid-photo-series-exposes-deep-racial-divide-New-York -nannies-young-wards.html.

4. "Meet Noreen," on Noreen Raines's website, accessed May 6, 2021, http://www .noreenraines.com/meet-noreen/.

5. Maya Salam, "For Serena Williams, Childbirth Was a Harrowing Ordeal. She's Not Alone," *New York Times*, January 11, 2018, https://www.nytimes.com/2018 /01/11/sports/tennis/serena-williams-baby-vogue.html.

6. Nina Martin and Renee Montagne, "Black Mothers Keep Dying after Giving Birth. Shalon Irving's Story Explains Why," *All Things Considered*, NPR, December 8, 2017, https://www.npr.org/2017/12/07/568948782/black-mothers -keep-dying-after-giving-birth-shalon-irvings-story-explains-why.

7. Jamie Nesbitt Golden, interview by author, December 22, 2020.

8. Beata Mostafavi, "Understanding Racial Disparities for Women with Uterine Fibroids," *Michigan Health Lab* (blog), University of Michigan, August 12, 2020, https://labblog.uofmhealth.org/rounds/understanding-racial-disparities-for -women-uterine-fibroids.

9. J. A. Martin et al., *Births: Final Data for 2018*, National Vital Statistics Reports, vol. 68, no. 13 (Hyattsville, MD: National Center for Health Statistics, 2019).

10. David Edwards, "George Will: Single Moms More Dangerous for Minorities than a Lack of Rights," Raw Story, December 9, 2020, https://www.rawstory .com/2013/08/george-will-single-moms-more-dangerous-for-minorities-than -a-lack-of-rights/.

11. Jimi Izrael, *The Denzel Principle: Why Black Women Can't Find Good Black Men* (New York: St. Martin's, 2010), 21.

12. Sarah Jackson, interview by author, November 2, 2012.

13. Ian Haney-Lopez, "The Racism at the Heart of the Reagan Presidency," *Salon*, January 11, 2014, http://www.salon.com/2014/01/11/the_racism_at_the_heart _of_the_reagan_presidency/.

14. Gene Demby, "The Truth behind the Lies of the Original 'Welfare Queen,'" *All Things Considered*, NPR, December 20, 2013, http://www.npr.org/blogs /codeswitch/2013/12/20/255819681/the-truth-behind-the-lies-of-the-original -welfare-queen.

15. Adam Liptak, "Supreme Court Ruling Makes Same-Sex Marriage a Right Nationwide," *New York Times*, June 26, 2015, https://www.nytimes.com/2015 /06/27/us/supreme-court-same-sex-marriage.html.

16. Gaby Galvin, "U.S. Marriage Rate Drops to a Record Low," *U.S. News & World Report*, April 29, 2020, https://www.usnews.com/news/healthiest-communities/articles/2020-04-29/us-marriage-rate-drops-to-record-low.

17. US Census Bureau, "For Young Adults, Cohabitation Is Up, Marriage Is Down," August 18, 2020, https://www.census.gov/library/stories/2018/11/cohabitaiton-is-up-marriage-is-down-for-young-adults.html.

18. Olga Khazan, "The Rise of Older Mothers," *Atlantic*, May 23, 2018, https://www.theatlantic.com/health/archive/2018/05/the-rise-of-older-mothers/560555/.

19. Khazan, "Rise of Older Mothers."

20. Sarah Jane Glynn, "Breadwinning Mothers Continue to Be the U.S. Norm," Center for American Progress, May 10, 2019, https://www.americanprogress.org/issues/women/reports/2019/05/10/469739/breadwinning-mothers-continue-u-s-norm/.

21. "The American Family Today," Pew Research Center's Social & Demographic Trends Project, Pew Research Center, May 30, 2020, https://www.pewresearch.org/social-trends/2015/12/17/1-the-american-family-today/.

22. Mary Parke, *Are Married Parents Really Better for Children?* (Washington, DC: Center for Law and Social Policy, 2003), http://www.clasp.org/resources-and-publications/states/0086.pdf.

23. Stacia Brown, interview by author, June 28, 2014.

24. Amina Khan, "Getting Killed by Police Is a Leading Cause of Death for Young Black Men in America," *Los Angeles Times*, August 16, 2019, https://www.latimes.com/science/story/2019-08-15/police-shootings-are-a-leading-cause-of-death-for-black-men; "Flint Water Crisis Fast Facts," CNN, January 14, 2021, https://www.cnn.com/2016/03/04/us/flint-water-crisis-fast-facts/index.html.

25. Jonathan Landrum Jr., "Aretha Franklin Funeral Eulogy Slammed; Pastor Stands Firm," Associated Press, September 2, 2018, https://apnews.com/article/32d797c5a5324c7593b44a6d0a1c8f3d.

26. Heidi Renée Lewis, interview by author, September 20, 2014.

27. Ta-Nehisi Coates, "Understanding Out-of-Wedlock Births in Black America," *Atlantic*, June 21, 2013, http://www.theatlantic.com/sexes/archive/2013/06/understanding-out-of-wedlock-births-in-Black-america/277084/.

28. Jim Rutenberg, "Fox Forced to Address Michelle Obama Headline," *New York Times*, June 12, 2008, http://thecaucus.blogs.nytimes.com/2008/06/12/fox-apologizes-for-michelle-obama-headline/?_php=true&_type=blogs&_r=0.

29. Yvette Perry, interview by author, June 24, 2014.

30. Brandee Mimitzraiem, interview by author, July 29, 2014.

31. Jennifer Kongs, "Interview with Tanya Fields: Urban Farming and Food Sovereignty Activist," *Mother Earth News*, October 28, 2014, https://www.motherearthnews.com/real-food/interview-tanya-fields-zboz1410zkon.

32. Brandi Summers, interview by author, July 11, 2014.

33. DeShong Perry Smitherman, interview by author, Indianapolis, December 15, 2014.

34. Deesha Philyaw, "Ain't I a Mommy," *Bitch*, Summer 2008, 46.

35. Michelle Hughes, interview by author, July 25, 2014.

Chapter 5: Anger: Twist and Shout

1. Alessandra Stanley, "Wrought in Rhimes's Image," *New York Times*, September 18, 2014, http://www.nytimes.com/2014/09/21/arts/television/viola-davis-plays-shonda-rhimess-latest-tough-heroine.html?_r=0.
2. Alexandra Ossola, "The Different Ways Black and White Women See Stereotypes in STEM," *Atlantic*, November 24, 2014, http://www.theatlantic.com/education/archive/2014/11/Black-girls-stand-a-better-chance-in-stem/383094/.
3. "Our Company," Bunim/Murray Productions, https://www.bunim-murray.com/about.
4. Bill Bradley, "Watch Porsha Williams Fight Kenya Moore on 'The Real Housewives of Atlanta' Reunion," *Huffington Post*, April 25, 2014, http://www.huffingtonpost.com/2014/04/21/real-housewives-fight_n_5187568.html.
5. Michael Arceneaux, "Love & Hip Hop Atlanta Reunion Recap, Part 2: 'Joseline All On They Mouth like Likka,'" Complex, September 2, 2014, http://www.complex.com/music/2014/09/love-and-hip-hop-atlanta-reunion-part-2.
6. Jennifer L. Pozner, *Reality Bites Back: The Troubling Truth about Guilty Pleasure TV* (Berkeley, CA: Seal Press, 2010), loc. 755 of 7725.
7. Pozner, *Reality Bites Back*, loc. 2655 of 7725.
8. Philip Caulfield, "'Sharkeisha' Fight Video Sickens Victim's Family after It Goes Viral; Teen Who Threw Violent Punches Arrested," *New York Daily News*, December 10, 2013, http://www.nydailynews.com/news/national/family-sickened-viral-fight-video-attacker-sharkeisha-arrested-article-1.1542354.
9. Gloria Pruitt, interview by author, July 1, 2014.
10. Ken Layne, "Mythological 'Whitey' Tape Will Finally Ruin Obama," Wonkette, June 2, 2008, http://wonkette.com/400121/mythological-whitey-tape-will-finally-ruin-obama.
11. Andy Soltis, "Michelle Not Amused by Obama's Memorial Selfie," *New York Post*, December 10, 2013, http://nypost.com/2013/12/10/michelle-annoyed-by-obamas-selfie-at-mandela-memorial/.
12. Liz Hurston, email message to author, September 25, 2014.
13. Kimberly Hopson, interview by author, September 12, 2014.
14. *Black Women in the United States, 2014*, National Coalition on Black Civic Participation and Black Women's Roundtable, v.
15. Tracy Elba, interview by author, September 25, 2014.

Chapter 6: Strength: Precious Mettle

1. Tamara Winfrey-Harris, "Precious Mettle," *Bitch*, Summer 2014, 40–43.
2. Charli Penn, "Exclusive: Robin Thicke on Love, Sex and Marriage," *Essence*, December 21, 2011, https://www.essence.com/news/robin-thicke-on-loving-black-women-interracial-dating-and-pleasing-paula/.
3. *Black Women in the United States, 2014*, National Coalition on Black Civic Participation and Black Women's Roundtable, v.
4. Deborah Latham-White, correspondence with author, December 2013.
5. Adrianne Traylor, correspondence with author, December 2013.

6. Fatima Thomas, interview by author, August 30, 2014.

7. Linda Arntzenius, "Abstract Expressionism and Prose Poetry When Baker Street Social Club Presents Danny Simmons," *Town Topics*, accessed December 10, 2014, http://www.towntopics.com/wordpress/2014/12/03/abstract -expressionism-and-prose-poetry-when-baker-street-social-club-presents -danny-simmons/.

8. Lisa Patton, interview by author, July 2, 2014.

9. Caroline Bird, "Black Woman Power," *New York* magazine, March 10, 1969, 36.

10. Mia Moody, Bruce Dorries, and Harriet Blackwell, "The Invisible Damsel: Differences in How National Media Outlets Framed the Coverage of Missing Black and White Women in the Mid-2000s," paper presented at the annual meeting of the International Communication Association, Montreal, Quebec, Canada, May 2008, http://www.academia.edu/944503/The_Invisible_Damsel _Differences_in_How_National_Media_Outlets_Framed_the_Coverage_of _Missing_Black_and_White_Women_in_the_Mid-2000s.

11. *Anderson Cooper 360°*, CNN, transcript, March 13, 2006.

12. Howard Koplowitz, "Glenda Moore, Staten Island Mother Who Lost 2 Sons in Hurricane Sandy, Returns to Site of Tragedy," *International Business Times*, November 2, 2012, http://www.ibtimes.com/glenda-moore-staten-island -mother-who-lost-2-sons-hurricane-sandy-returns-site-tragedy-858289.

13. Sami K. Martin, "Glenda Moore 'Wailed Uncontrollably' after Police Identified Sons Swept Away by Sandy," *Christian Post*, November 2, 2012, http://www .christianpost.com/news/glenda-moore-wailed-uncontrollably-after-police -identified-sons-swept-away-by-sandy-84323/.

14. Mary M. Chapman, "Theodore Wafer Sentenced to 17 Years in Michigan Shooting of Renisha McBride," *New York Times*, September 3, 2014, http://www .nytimes.com/2014/09/04/us/theodore-wafer-sentenced-in-killing-of-renisha -mcbride.html.

15. DJ Freedom Fighter, "Critically Analyzing Glenda Moore's Story through Optic Whiteness," DJ Freedom Fighter, http://djfreedomfighter.tumblr.com/post /35078117848/critically-analyzing-glenda-moores-story-through-optic (site discontinued).

16. Noliwe M. Rooks, "Renisha McBride and Evolution of Black-Female Stereo- type," *Time*, November 14, 2013, http://ideas.time.com/2013/11/14/renisha -mcbride-and-Black-female-stereotype/.

17. Richard A. Oppel, Derrick Bryson Taylor, and Nicholas Bogel-Burroughs, "What to Know about Breonna Taylor's Death," *New York Times*, May 30, 2020, https://www.nytimes.com/article/breonna-taylor-police.html#:~:text=The%20 death%20of%20Breonna%20Taylor,injustice%20in%20the%20United%20 States.

18. Kimberlé Williams Crenshaw et al., *Say Her Name: Resisting Police Brutality against Black Women* (New York: African American Policy Forum, 2015).

19. Joseph Diaz et al., "Ex-Oklahoma City Cop Spending 263 Years in Prison for Rape and His Accusers Share Their Stories," ABC News, April 21, 2016, https://abcnews.go.com/US/oklahoma-city-cop-spending-263-years-prison- rape/story?id=38517467.

20. Jason Johnson, "The Holtzclaw Trial: When Rape Culture Meets #BlackLives-Matter," NBCNews.com, November 13, 2015, https://www.nbcnews.com/news/nbcblk/holtzclaw-trial-when-rape-culture-meets-blacklivesmatter-n458741.

21. S. E. James et al., *The Report of the 2015 U.S. Transgender Survey* (Washington, DC: National Center for Transgender Equality, 2016).

22. Alisha Haridasani Gupta, "Since 2015: 48 Black Women Killed by the Police. And Only 2 Charges," *New York Times*, September 24, 2020, https://www.nytimes.com/2020/09/24/us/breonna-taylor-grand-jury-black-women.html.

23. Eliott C. McLaughlin, "An Officer Was Indicted for Endangering Neighbors, but Not Breonna Taylor, with His Bullets. This May Be Why," CNN, October 1, 2020, https://www.cnn.com/2020/10/01/us/legal-analysis-breonna-taylor-grand-jury/index.html.

24. "#SayHerName In Memoriam," African American Policy Forum, accessed March 18, 2021, https://www.aapf.org/in-memorium.

25. Crenshaw et al., *Say Her Name.*

26. "About #SAY HER NAME," African American Policy Forum, 2014, https://www.aapf.org/sayhername.

27. "Herstory," Black Lives Matter, September 7, 2019, https://blacklivesmatter.com/herstory/.

28. Nada Hassanein, "Florida Protester Oluwatoyin Salau Killed in Tallahassee after Going Missing," *Tallahassee Democrat*, June 16, 2020, https://www.tallahassee.com/story/news/2020/06/15/oluwatoyin-salau-found-dead-tallahassee-black-lives-matter-protest-missing/3190021001/.

29. Giulia McDonnell Nieto, "Oluwatoyin Salau, Missing Black Lives Matter Activist, Is Found Dead," *New York Times*, June 15, 2020, https://www.nytimes.com/2020/06/15/us/oluwatoyin-salau-dead-aaron-glee.html.

30. "Meet Our Founder," Outdoor Afro, https://outdoorafro.com/team/.

31. Sofia Quintero, correspondence with author, January 29, 2014.

Chapter 7: Health: Fat, Sick, and Crazy

1. National Center for Health Statistics, *Health, United States, 2013: With Special Feature on Prescription Drugs* (Hyattsville, MD: National Center for Health Statistics, 2014).

2. S. S. Rajaram and V. Vinson, "African American Women and Diabetes: A Sociocultural Context," *Journal of Health Care for the Poor and Underserved* 9, no. 3 (1998): 236–47, https://doi.org/10.1353/hpu.2010.0321.

3. US Department of Health and Human Services and National Institutes of Health, *The Heart Truth for Women*, NIH Publication No. 07-5066 (Washington, DC: originally printed September 2003, revised July 2009).

4. US Department of Health and Human Services and National Institutes of Health, *The Heart Truth.*

5. Erica Martin Richards, "Mental Health among African-American Women," Johns Hopkins Medicine, accessed May 1, 2021, https://www.hopkinsmedicine.org/health/wellness-and-prevention/mental-health-among-african-american-women.

6. O. Kenrik Duru et al., "Allostatic Load Burden and Racial Disparities in Mortality," *Journal of the National Medical Association* 104, no. 1–2 (January–February 2012), https://doi.org/10.1016/S0027-9684(15)30120-6.

7. Esther Gross, Victoria Efetevbia, and Alexandra Wilkins, "Racism and Sexism against Black Women May Contribute to High Rates of Black Infant Mortality," Child Trends, April 9, 2020, https://www.childtrends.org/blog/racism-sexism-against-black-women-may-contribute-high-rates-black-infant-mortality.

8. Alissa Greenberg, "How the Stress of Racism Can Harm Your Health—And What That Has to Do with Covid-19," PBS, July 14, 2020, https://www.pbs.org/wgbh/nova/article/racism-stress-covid-allostatic-load/.

9. "Risk for COVID-19 Infection, Hospitalization, and Death by Race/Ethnicity," Centers for Disease Control and Prevention, March 12, 2021, https://www.cdc.gov/coronavirus/2019-ncov/covid-data/investigations-discovery/hospitalization-death-by-race-ethnicity.html.

10. Raquel E. Gur et al., "The Disproportionate Burden of the COVID-19 Pandemic among Pregnant Black Women," US National Library of Medicine National Institutes of Health, November 2020, https://www.ncbi.nlm.nih.gov/pmc/articles/PMC7513921/.

11. O. Kenrik Duru et al., "Allostatic Load Burden."

12. Deborah Latham-White interview.

13. "About," The Nap Ministry, January 7, 2021, https://thenapministry.wordpress.com/about/.

14. Adele Jackson-Gibson, "The Racist and Problematic Origins of the Body Mass Index," *Good Housekeeping*, March 2, 2021, https://www.goodhousekeeping.com/health/diet-nutrition/a35047103/bmi-racist-history/.

15. Sabrina Strings, essay in *Fearing the Black Body: the Racial Origins of Fat Phobia* (New York: New York University Press, 2019), 6.

16. Erika Nicole Kendall, "On @BorisKodjoe's Twitter Rant about Obesity," Black Girl's Guide to Weight Loss, August 19, 2004, http://Blackgirlsguidetoweightloss.com/celeb-watch/boriskodjoes-twitter-rant-about-obesity/.

17. Erika Nicole Kendall, interview by author, August 26, 2014.

18. Paula Dutko, Michele Ver Ploeg, and Tracey Farrigan, *Characteristics and Influential Factors of Food Deserts*, Economic Research Report Number 140 (Washington, DC: United States Department of Agriculture, 2012).

19. "Toni Carey and Ashley Hicks of Black Girls Run! Give the Skinny on Their Nationwide Movement," Black Enterprise, October 8, 2012, https://www.blackenterprise.com/toni-carey-and-ashley-hicks-of-black-girls-run-give-the-skinny-on-their-nationwide-movement/.

20. "Black Women Avoiding Exercise to Maintain Hairstyles: Study," Reuters, *Huffington Post*, December 18, 2012, http://www.huffingtonpost.com/2012/12/18/Black-women-hair-avoid-exercise_n_2321539.html?ncid=edlinkusaolp00000003.

21. "Overweight and Obesity," Centers for Disease Control and Prevention, page last reviewed February 11, 2021, http://www.cdc.gov/obesity/data/adult.html.

22. Dr. Virginia Banks Bright, interview by author, November 21, 2014.

23. Earlise C. Ward and Susan M. Heidrich, "African American Women's Beliefs about Mental Illness, Stigma, and Preferred Coping Behaviors," *Research in*

Nursing and Health 32, no. 5 (October 2009): 480–92, https://doi.org/10.1002 /nur.20344.

24. Adrianne Traylor, interview by author, August 17, 2014.

25. Suncear Scretchen, "Yogapreneur: Nikki Myers Recharges Life with 12-Step Yoga Program," Black Enterprise, http://www.Blackenterprise.com/lifestyle /nikki-myers-yoga-12-step-program/.

26. Adrianne Traylor interview.

27. Vivian St. Claire, interview by author, June 29, 2014.

Chapter 8: Power: Fuck It, I'll Do It!

1. P. R. Lockhart, "Black Women Turned Electoral Power into Political Power in 2018," Vox, November 9, 2018, https://www.vox.com/identities/2018/11 /9/18079046/black-women-candidates-history-midterm-elections.

2. Julie Hinds and Chanel Stitt, "VP Pick Kamala Harris, an AKA and HBCU Grad, Connects with Black Community on Many Levels," *Detroit Free Press*, August 17, 2020, https://www.freep.com/story/news/politics/elections /2020/08/16/kamala-harris-aka-hbcu-grad-connects-black-community /3374026001/.

3. P. R. Lockhart, "Will Virginia Stay Blue? It Depends on Black Turnout on Tuesday," *Mother Jones*, October 18, 2017, https://www.motherjones.com/ politics/2017/10/will-virginia-stay-blue-it-depends-on-black-turnout-next -month/; Astead W. Herndon, "Georgia Was a Big Win for Democrats. Black Women Did the Groundwork," *New York Times*, December 3, 2020, https://www .nytimes.com/2020/12/03/us/politics/georgia-democrats-black-women.html.

4. "Get to Know Us: Tarana Burke, Founder," me too. Movement, July 17, 2020, https://metoomvmt.org/get-to-know-us/tarana-burke-founder/.

5. Halimah, interview by author, December 3, 2020.

6. Jessica Louise, interview by author, December 9, 2020.

7. Madison Feller, Savannah Walsh, and Hilary Weaver, "Layleen Polanco's Family Will Receive Record $5.9 Million Settlement a Year after Her Death at Rikers," *Elle*, September 3, 2020, https://www.elle.com/culture/career-politics/a27921290 /who-is-layleen-polanco-transgender-woman-died-solitary-confinement/.

8. Jeanne Theoharis, "How Women's Voices Were Excluded from the March," MSNBC, September 24, 2020, https://www.msnbc.com/melissa-harris-perry /how-womens-voices-were-excluded-the-msna155781.

9. Dalvin Brown, "Marsha P. Johnson: Transgender Hero of Stonewall Riots Finally Gets Her Due," *USA Today*, June 28, 2019, https://www.usatoday.com /story/news/investigations/2019/03/27/black-history-marsha-johnson-and- stonewall-riots/2353538002/.

10. Bianca Mac, interview by author, December 15, 2020.

11. Astead W. Herndon and Annie Karni, "Biden Leads, but No Call Yet Four Days after Election: This Week in the 2020 Race," *New York Times*, November 7, 2020, https://www.nytimes.com/2020/11/07/us/politics/the-election.html.

12. Jonathan Martin and Alexander Burns, "Biden Wins Presidency, Ending Four Tumultuous Years under Trump," *New York Times*, November 7, 2020, https:// www.nytimes.com/2020/11/07/us/politics/biden-election.html.

13. Herndon, "Georgia Was a Big Win."

14. "National Exit Polls: How Different Groups Voted," *New York Times*, January 5, 2021, https://www.nytimes.com/interactive/2020/11/03/us/elections/exit-polls -president.html.

15. Katanga Johnson and Heather Timmons, "How Stacey Abrams Paved the Way for a Democratic Victory in 'New Georgia,'" Reuters, November 9, 2020, https:// www.reuters.com/article/usa-election-georgia/how-stacey-abrams-paved-the -way-for-a-democratic-victory-in-new-georgia-idUSKBN27P197.

16. Ben Nadler, "Georgia Republican Candidate for Governor Puts 53,000 Voter Registrations on Hold," *USA Today*, October 12, 2018, https://www.usatoday .com/story/news/politics/elections/2018/10/11/georgia-republican-candidate -brian-kemp-puts-53-000-voter-registrations-hold/1608507002/.

17. Courtney Connley, "How Stacey Abrams, LaTosha Brown and Other Black Women Changed the Course of the 2020 Election," CNBC, November 6, 2020, https://www.cnbc.com/2020/11/06/black-women-continue-to-be-the-democratic -partys-most-powerful-weapon.html.

18. Connley, "Stacey Abrams, LaTosha Brown."

19. "Former Georgia Gubernatorial Candidate on a Push for Voter Turnout," *All Things Considered*, NPR, November 2, 2020, https://www.npr.org/2020/11/02 /930504055/former-georgia-gubernatorial-candidate-on-a-push-for-voter -turnout.

20. Richard Fausset, Jonathan Martin, and Reid J. Epstein, "Georgia Highlights: Democrats Win the Senate as Ossoff Defeats Perdue," *New York Times*, January 8, 2021, https://www.nytimes.com/live/2021/01/06/us/georgia-election-results.

21. Herndon, "Georgia Was a Big Win."

22. Martha Jones, "Opinion: Black Women Voters Changed the Shape of the U.S. Election. It's Time to Thank Them," Thomson Reuters Foundation, November 12, 2020, https://news.trust.org/item/20201112173512-en64k/.

23. Erin Canty, "15 Real Ways to Thank Black Women for Carrying the Country on Their Backs," Upworthy, April 15, 2020, https://www.upworthy.com/15-real -ways-to-thank-black-women-for-carrying-the-country-on-their-backs.

24. Kate Rushin, "Poem of the Day 'The Bridge Poem,'" Trinity College of Arts & Sciences, English Department, Duke University, June 28, 2020, https://english .duke.edu/news/poem-day-bridge-poem.

25. Jennifer Wright, "Kamala Harris Is Already Being Called a Prostitute," *Harper's Bazaar*, January 29, 2019, https://www.harpersbazaar.com/culture/politics /a26077919/kamala-harris-willie-brown-dating-explained/; Maggie Astor, "Kamala Harris Faced a Double Standard on the Debate Stage," *New York Times*, October 8, 2020, https://www.nytimes.com/2020/10/07/us/politics/kamala -harris-faced-a-double-standard-on-the-debate-stage.html.

26. Asma Khalid, "Pressure Grows on Joe Biden to Pick a Black Woman as His Running Mate," NPR, June 12, 2020, https://www.npr.org/2020/06/12/875000650 /pressure-grows-on-joe-biden-to-pick-a-black-woman-as-his-running-mate.

27. Adia Winfrey, interview by author, December 15, 2020.

28. Jasmine Lee et al., "Alabama Election Results: Doug Jones Defeats Roy Moore in U.S. Senate Race," *New York Times*, December 12, 2017, https://www.nytimes .com/elections/results/alabama-senate-special-election-roy-moore-doug-jones;

Krista Gmelich, "Republicans Flip Alabama Senate Seat as Tuberville Beats Jones," *Bloomberg*, November 3, 2020, https://www.bloomberg.com/news /articles/2020-11-04/republicans-flip-alabama-senate-seat-as-tuberville -beats-jones.

29. Jessica Louise, interview by author, December 9, 2020.

30. Bianca Mac, interview by author, December 15, 2020.

Epilogue: The Sisters Are Alright

1. "Washington Post–Kaiser Family Foundation Poll of Black Women in America," *Washington Post*, updated February 27, 2012, https://www.washingtonpost .com/wp-srv/special/nation/black-women-in-america/.

2. Ebony Murphy-Root, correspondence with author, September 29, 2014.

Acknowledgments

Bookish girls grow up dreaming of being published—at least this one did. The first edition of *The Sisters Are Alright* was a dream come true.

It would have been impossible without my parents, Joseph and Constance Winfrey, who gave me a love of words and a belief that I can do anything; my husband, LaMarl Harris, who graciously suffered the messy and all-consuming process of birthing the book; and my friends and fellow writers—Andrea Plaid, Christopher MacDonald-Dennis, Deesha Philyaw, Stephanie Gilmore, and Carolyn Edgar.

To my girls who supported me through this second go—Dr. Tyffani Monford Dent, Dr. Carolyn Strong, DeShong Perry Smitherman, Dr. LaTasha Sturdivant, Rochelle Riley, and always, Deesha Philyaw—y'all are the best!

And to the hundreds of women I interviewed for both editions of this book: I see you sparkling. Thank you for trusting me with your stories. I hope I did them justice.

Index

NUMBERS

About the Author

Tamara Winfrey-Harris is a writer who specializes in the ever-evolving space where current events, politics, and pop culture intersect with race and gender. She says, "I want to tell the stories of Black women and girls, and deliver the truth to all those folks who got us twisted—tangled up in racist and sexist lies. I want my writing to advocate for my sisters. We are better than alright. We are amazing."

Well versed on a range of topics, including Beyoncé's feminism, Rachel Dolezal's White privilege, and the Black church and female sexuality, Tamara has been published in media outlets including the *New York Times*, the *Atlantic*, *Cosmopolitan*, *New York* magazine, and the *Los Angeles Times*. And she has been called to share her analysis on media outlets, including NPR's *Weekend Edition* and Janet Mock's *So POPular!* on MSNBC.com, and on university campuses nationwide.

Tamara's first book, *The Sisters Are Alright: Changing the Broken Narrative of Black Women in America*, was published by Berrett-Koehler Publishers in 2015 and called "a myth-busting portrait of Black women in America" by the *Washington Post*. The book won the Phyllis Wheatley Award, IndieFab Award, Independent Publishers Living Now Award, and IPPY Award. Her second book, *Dear Black Girl: Letters from Your Sisters on Stepping into Your Power*, debuted in 2021.

Tamara's essays also appear in *The Lemonade Reader: Beyoncé, Black Feminism and Spirituality* (Routledge, 2019), *The Burden: African Americans and the Enduring Impact of Slavery* (Wayne State University Press, 2018), *Black in the Middle: An Anthology of the Black Midwest* (Black Belt Publishing, 2020), and other books.

Tamara is also the cofounder of Centering Sisters, LLC, an organization that unapologetically addresses the needs and issues of Black women, girls, and femmes.

In 2020, she completed her two-hundred-hour yoga teacher training and is certified RYT 200. Tamara says, "Yoga is not exercise; it is healing and liberation and beauty. I want to share that with people who are chronically disregarded and oppressed, wherever they are—at home, at school, in community centers. I especially want to do yoga with my sisters, because they deserve this peace."

Tamara is a native of Gary, Indiana, and a proud member of Alpha Kappa Alpha, Sorority, Inc. She graduated with a BA degree from the Greenlee School of Journalism at Iowa State University.

Also by Tamara Winfrey-Harris

Dear Black Girl

Letters From Your Sisters on Stepping Into Your Power

"Dear #DopeBlackGirl, You don't know me, but I know you. I know you because I am you! We are magic, light, and stars in the universe." So begins a letter that Tamara Winfrey Harris received as part of her Letters to Black Girls project, where she asked Black women to write honest, open, and inspiring letters of support to young Black girls aged thirteen to twenty-one. In *Dear Black Girl*, Winfrey Harris organizes a selection of these feminist, anti-racist, body positive, LGBTQ+ positive, anti-respectability politics, and pro-Black letters, modeling how Black women can nurture future generations. Each chapter ends with a prompt encouraging girls to write a letter to themselves, teaching the art of self-love and self-nurturing.

Paperback, ISBN 978-1-5230-9229-1
PDF ebook, ISBN 978-1-5230-9230-7
ePub ebook, ISBN 978-1-5230-9231-4
Digital audiobook 978-1-5230-9232-1

BK® Berrett–Koehler Publishers, Inc.
www.bkconnection.com

800.929.2929

Berrett–Koehler
BK Publishers

Berrett-Koehler is an independent publisher dedicated to an ambitious mission: *Connecting people and ideas to create a world that works for all.*

Our publications span many formats, including print, digital, audio, and video. We also offer online resources, training, and gatherings. And we will continue expanding our products and services to advance our mission.

We believe that the solutions to the world's problems will come from all of us, working at all levels: in our society, in our organizations, and in our own lives. Our publications and resources offer pathways to creating a more just, equitable, and sustainable society. They help people make their organizations more humane, democratic, diverse, and effective (and we don't think there's any contradiction there). And they guide people in creating positive change in their own lives and aligning their personal practices with their aspirations for a better world.

And we strive to practice what we preach through what we call "The BK Way." At the core of this approach is *stewardship,* a deep sense of responsibility to administer the company for the benefit of all of our stakeholder groups, including authors, customers, employees, investors, service providers, sales partners, and the communities and environment around us. Everything we do is built around stewardship and our other core values of *quality, partnership, inclusion,* and *sustainability.*

This is why Berrett-Koehler is the first book publishing company to be both a B Corporation (a rigorous certification) and a benefit corporation (a for-profit legal status), which together require us to adhere to the highest standards for corporate, social, and environmental performance. And it is why we have instituted many pioneering practices (which you can learn about at www.bkconnection.com), including the Berrett-Koehler Constitution, the Bill of Rights and Responsibilities for BK Authors, and our unique Author Days.

We are grateful to our readers, authors, and other friends who are supporting our mission. We ask you to share with us examples of how BK publications and resources are making a difference in your lives, organizations, and communities at www.bkconnection.com/impact.

Dear reader,

Thank you for picking up this book and welcome to the worldwide BK community! You're joining a special group of people who have come together to create positive change in their lives, organizations, and communities.

What's BK all about?

Our mission is to connect people and ideas to create a world that works for all.

Why? Our communities, organizations, and lives get bogged down by old paradigms of self-interest, exclusion, hierarchy, and privilege. But we believe that can change. That's why we seek the leading experts on these challenges—and share their actionable ideas with you.

A welcome gift

To help you get started, we'd like to offer you a **free copy** of one of our bestselling ebooks:

www.bkconnection.com/welcome

When you claim your **free ebook**, you'll also be subscribed to our blog.

Our freshest insights

Access the best new tools and ideas for leaders at all levels on our blog at ideas.bkconnection.com.

Sincerely,

Your friends at Berrett-Koehler